'Ben Furman has done it again – created a step-by-step guide through the tougher regions of effective parenting. The concept is elegantly simple: for every challenge that faces a child or young person, whether it be difficulty sleeping, temper tantrums or dealing with life's difficulties, there will be a skill that the child can learn and with this skill overcome the challenge. The idea is as practical as it is elegant but to follow it through is not so easy. What Dr Furman does in this book is teach parents the skill they need to identify the skills their children need in order to live more happy and fulfilling lives. These skills are not obvious and need considerable negotiation between the child and concerned adults: the child who curses learns the "teddy bear" skill while another, prone to meltdowns, develops the "helping hand" skill. The key is not to stop the unwanted behaviour but to replace it with something new. This may take time, there is no claim to have a "magic bullet", but it focuses attention away from the problem ("Don't do that!") to a more positive future ("Remember your new skill!") This focus on what is desired rather than on unwanted behaviours is less stressful and more hopeful for children and parents alike and anything that makes life easier is to be welcomed! What also makes life easier is the contents page of the book where Dr Furman's 50+ detailed examples make finding the page that fits your child very easy: Nightmares 122, Screen time 134, Shyness, 139 and so on; almost everything covered and as no child will have more than a few of these challenges it is a good book to share with friends whose children also need new skills.'

Chris Iveson, *co-founder of BRIEF London, one of the world's leading centres for Solution Focused training*

'A child rearing guide – what a scary term. Fortunately, for Ben Furman this new book isn't a child rearing guide, but rather a book that provides ideas for skills-based parenting from an experienced teacher and author. The book is good, as one might expect. It concretely covers, among other things, picky eating, low self-esteem, attention difficulties, tantrums, bullying, anxiety, selective mutism, violence, and divorce. The book also discusses skill-based education in schools and how to improve collaboration with students and parents. There is hardly anyone who would not benefit from this book, even if they are not a parent, grandparent, or teacher. And in case you should find Furman's gentle and explanatory style somewhat fluffy or unduly optimistic, don't be alarmed. There is enough anxiety and pessimism around to warrant the ideas of Dr Ben Furman.'

Heli Mustonen, *freelance journalist,*
Finland

THE SOLUTION-FOCUSED PARENT

This practical book presents readers with a skills-based, child rearing approach to supporting a child's growth and helping them overcome both minor and major developmental challenges.

In contrast to conventional approaches to child psychology, this innovative approach focuses on developing children's abilities rather than concentrating on and trying to fix their "problems." Additionally, instead of blaming caretakers for their child's challenges, the skills approach offers them the keys with which they can coach and motivate their children to overcome challenges by learning required skills. Readers will find it easy to grasp the idea of the skills mindset through the book's wealth of eye-opening stories, case examples, and the author's personal insights as a psychotherapist, parent, and creator of the Kids'Skills method. Clear, detailed instructions will help readers immediately put the ideas into everyday practice with their own children and families.

This book is a must-have, hope-instilling toolbox for anyone involved in the task of raising a child. Parents, grandparents, teachers, mental health professionals, and more will find this a valuable resource in ensuring the future success of the children in their lives.

Dr Ben Furman is a renowned Finnish psychiatrist, author, and teacher of solution-focused therapy and coaching. He founded the Helsinki Brief Therapy Institute in 1986 together with his long-time colleague, Tapani Ahola, where he and his team have provided training in solution-focused psychology for professionals ever since.

He has authored more than 30 books about solution-focused psychology, many of which he has written together with Tapani Ahola. One of his most well-known books, *It's Never Too Late to Have a Happy Childhood*, was published in 1997 and has been translated into 10 languages.

At the turn of the century, Dr Furman became widely known in his home country for hosting a psychology talk show on national TV that bore his own name. The program aired for several years and generated 200 episodes in total.

Dr Furman is an internationally acclaimed teacher of solution-focused therapy. He has spoken and taught in many countries around the world and his books have appeared in 25 languages.

For more information about Dr Furman, his books, and other products, visit his website at www.benfurman.com

THE SOLUTION-FOCUSED PARENT

How to Help Children Conquer Challenges by Learning Skills

Ben Furman

Routledge
Taylor & Francis Group

LONDON AND NEW YORK

Designed cover image: © Illustration Kai Kujasalo

First published in English 2024
by Routledge
4 Park Square, Milton Park, Abingdon, Oxon OX14 4RN

and by Routledge
605 Third Avenue, New York, NY 10158

Routledge is an imprint of the Taylor & Francis Group, an informa business

Ben Furman & Lasten haasteet taidoiksi

Copyright © 2023 Ben Furman

First published in Finland in 2023 by Viisas Elämä

British Library Cataloguing-in-Publication Data
A catalogue record for this book is available from the British Library

Library of Congress Cataloging-in-Publication Data
Names: Furman, Ben, author.
Title: The solution-focused parent: how to help children conquer challenges by learning skills/Ben Furman.
Other titles: Ben Furman & lasten haasteet taidoiksi. English
Description: First English edition. | Abingdon, Oxon; New York, NY: Routledge, 2024. | "First published in Finland as Ben Furman & lasten haasteet taidoiksi in 2023 by Viisas Elämä"—Title page verso.
Identifiers: LCCN 2023026989 (print) | LCCN 2023026990 (ebook) | ISBN 9781032564807 (hardback) | ISBN 9781032564791 (paperback) | ISBN 9781003435723 (ebook)
Subjects: LCSH: Child rearing. | Parenting. | Child development.
Classification: LCC HQ772 .F87 2024 (print) | LCC HQ772 (ebook) | DDC 649.1—dc23/eng/20230713
LC record available at https://lccn.loc.gov/2023026989
LC ebook record available at https://lccn.loc.gov/2023026990

ISBN: 9781032564807 (hbk)
ISBN: 9781032564791 (pbk)
ISBN: 9781003435723 (ebk)

DOI: 10.4324/9781003435723

Typeset in Chaparral
by Deanta Global Publishing Services, Chennai, India

CONTENTS

ACKNOWLEDGEMENTS

I wish to acknowledge my long-time colleague Tapani with whom I have developed over the past four decades several applications of solution-focused psychology and special education teachers Sirpa Birn and Tuija Terävä (†2022) for collaborating with me in developing the Kids'Skills approach. In addition, I want to thank also Elizabeth Puller for helping me with English language and my editor Grace McDonnell at the Taylor and Francis publishing house.

Photo by Leon Liu on Unsplash

1

THE RHYME STONE TALE

DOI: 10.4324/9781003435723-1

My intention with this book is to familiarise you with what I like to call the skills approach to parenting and child-rearing. It is a creative and enjoyable way to facilitate children's growth and help them overcome challenges by learning new skills. The basic idea of the skills approach is easy to grasp, and by the time you finish reading this book, if you feel that the approach matches your own values and thinking, you will be able to start putting the ideas into practice straight away with your own child, or the children you care for.

Before I go on to explain to you in detail what I mean by the skills approach and how you can use it with your children, I would like to start by telling you a tale as an intro to the approach described in the book. If you are not a great fan of this kind of allegorical story, feel free to skip the next few pages and start from Chapter 2.

Once upon a time, in a faraway village, strange things had begun to happen. The children in the village had started to develop all sorts of mysterious problems. Some children had suddenly become so shy that they were unable to utter any words, and others had become so irritated that they swung around aimlessly hitting other people. Some had started to fear things when there was nothing to be afraid of, and still others had developed peculiar sticky habits they couldn't get rid of despite all their parents' efforts, like plucking their hair or sucking their fingers..

The elders in the village were summoned to discuss the situation. "We have to find out what is the cause of this thorny problem," said one of elders. This sparked a conversation that lasted for a long time. Soon the entire village was feverishly deliberating over what was causing the children's problems.

At first, villagers suspected that the children's problems were caused by poisoned water. For this reason, the villagers started to carry water to the village all the way from the neighbouring village. However, that didn't help. The next suspicion was that the children's problems were caused by the children having been frightened about something when they were infants. Based on this idea, the villagers started to do their utmost to protect the children from ever getting frightened, but that turned out to be very difficult because in those days life was hazardous and preventing children from ever being frightened was practically impossible. Someone came along and proposed that the children's many problems were caused by incompetent parenting. It was suggested that for some unknown reason the parents had lost their ability to raise their children. Based on this idea, the parents were mandated to take classes where the elders taught them how to properly raise their children. This, too, soon turned out to be a disappointment. The elders who taught the parents had so many disagreements about what the proper way was to raise children that their teaching only added to the villagers' confusion.

Villagers kept coming up with new explanations for what might be causing the children's problems, but the conundrum remained unsolved. Many villagers started to suspect that the many explanations that had been generated had, in fact, made matters worse. They had made the parents in the village feel blamed for the problems of their children. They had contributed to sadness and desperation.

When the villagers had been thinking about the children's problem for quite some time and the mood of the village had sunk, one of the elders proclaimed: "We have done our best to solve this predicament of ours, but we haven't succeeded in finding a solution. It is time for us to consult the Wise Wizard and let her advise us on the matter."

Three of the elders set out on foot to meet with the wizard. Having travelled a long distance, they arrived in the town where the wizard lived.

"A long time has passed since people from your village last came to consult me for advice," said the wizard. "What brings you to me this time?"

The elders described their predicament to the wizard and told her about all the various explanations that the villagers had come up with to account for the mysterious problems of the children. When they had spoken, the wizard lowered her gaze, closed her eyes, and appeared to fall asleep. After a while she opened her eyes again and spoke:

*Since the beginning of time
there's been problems and crime.
Focusing on explanations leads to blaming
which is no more than a road to shaming.*

*If your aim is problems to eliminate,
you are doomed to stalemate.
To help children back on track
find a skill for them to crack.*

When the three elders returned to the village, they asked the stonecutter to chisel the wizard's rhyme into a stone that stood at the centre of the village. The elders then gathered around the stone to decipher what the wizard meant to tell them with the rhyme.

Having pondered the words of the rhyme for a time, the elders summoned the villagers and told them:

"With this rhyme, the wizard wants to tell us that we need to cease looking for explanations to our children's problems and focus instead on discovering what skills they need to learn to conquer their problems."

The villagers were delighted with this message. They understood that it meant it was time to stop blaming themselves and others alike. From now on, time didn't need to be spent on disputing the causes of children's problems and everyone could focus on helping children develop the skills they needed to overcome their difficulties.

Villagers returned home and informed their children that from now on they would be learning skills to overcome their difficulties. The children were delighted to hear the news as they had grown all too tired of listening to their parents' endless speculations about the causes of their problems.

Villagers took action, and in no time each child in the village had a skill to learn that would help them to overcome their problem. At first things worked well, but a new problem soon loomed on the horizon. "We succeeded in making agreements with our children about skills to learn," the villagers lamented to the elders, "but when it was time for them to take action to learn those skills, they soon lost their interest, and we couldn't find a way to get them to make the effort to learn those skills. How are we supposed to get our children to learn their skills?"

Again, the elders sat down to think about the villagers' thorny question, but no matter how hard they tried, they couldn't find an answer. Finally, they decided to let the 3 elders visit the Wise Wizard again to ask for her advice.

"What brings you to me this time?" the wizard asked them upon their arrival.

The elders said: "When we consulted you last time, you advised us to give up our futile efforts to try to explain our children's problems and focus, instead, on finding out what skills they need to learn to conquer their problems. This is what we did, but now we are stuck and faced with a new challenge. We don't know how to get our children to take the steps and make the effort to learn the skills they need to learn."

The wizard listened to the elders attentively. She then lowered her gaze, closed her eyes, and appeared to fall asleep. When she opened her eyes again and lifted her gaze, she uttered the following words:

> For wanting a skill to learn
> you must see the things you earn.
> The list of benefits should be long
> like an unending lullaby song.
>
> Give your skill a name,
> to make learning it a game
> and find a magic friend,
> to accompany you till the end.
>
> No matter how easy it may seem,
> you will need a supporting team.
> They will form the crew
> who believe in you.
>
> Before long you'll be sure to stumble
> but that's no reason for you to tumble.
> Better ask your team to be kinder,
> by giving you a gentle reminder.
>
> With the help of your team
> you will soon reach your dream.
> To enjoy your new rank
> don't forget your team to thank.
>
> Weeks will roll and days will pass,
> how to make sure the skill will last?
> Teach your skill to someone else.
> That will do the trick
> and make sure your skill will stick.

The three elders memorized the words of the wizard and set off on foot to return to their village. Once they arrived in the village, they asked the stone mason to chisel the wizard's words into the stone at the centre of the village. The elders then gathered to discuss the wizard's words and soon announced their conclusion:

> "The wizard's rhyme is an answer to our question. It offers us directions on how to motivate our children to learn their skills. Let us follow its guidance and our predicament may soon belong to the past."

As the villagers started to follow the directions embedded in the wizard's rhyme, their children became keen on developing their skills, and as they learned their skills, one by one, they overcame their problems. And whenever the children stumbled upon any new difficulties later, those were also successfully handled with the wisdom of the rhyme in the stone. The villagers were relieved. The predicament had been conquered.

2

WHAT IS THE SKILLS
APPROACH?

DOI: 10.4324/9781003435723-2

T he skills approach is founded on the idea that children don't have problems; they just haven't learned some skills *yet*.

Children don't have problems,
they only have skills they haven't learned yet.

The skills approach emerged in the 90s in a kindergarten in Helsinki, Finland. The kindergarten had a special unit that cared for children with special needs. The unit was managed by two special education teachers, Sirpa Birn and Tuija Terävä. I worked with them for a few years as an external supervisor. When we started our collaboration, we decided to put our heads together to develop a widely applicable method to help children overcome emotional and behavioural challenges. Our idea was to try to generate a simple step-by-step method that both children and their parents would find appealing. We were influenced by solution-focused psychology[1], a therapeutic approach that I teach, but also by various methods of special education that the teachers were familiar with. Little by little, through trial and error, our collaboration led to the development of a hands-on method consisting of 15 practical steps that we ended up calling Kids'Skills. At that time, we had no idea that this brainchild of ours would in the coming years raise wide international

---

1 **The origins of the skills approach**

When I was specialising in psychiatry in the 80s practically all the professors of psychiatry and child psychiatry in my country, Finland, believed in psychoanalysis. It is a school of psychotherapy developed in the early 20th century by the Austrian neurologist Sigmund Freud, whose proponents believe that all mental health problems can be traced back to childhood experiences. Psychiatrists and child psychiatrists who represented psychoanalysis recommended intensive individual psychotherapy for almost all their patients, including children. At that time most of my peers, who were also specialising in psychiatry, opted to become psychoanalysts, but there were a few of us who were disillusioned with psychoanalytic doctrines and who had a burning desire to discover more effective means of helping our clients.

I became interested in family therapy in general and solution-focused brief therapy in particular. Solution-focused therapy emerged within the family therapy movement, and it was the new kid on the block at the time. Contrary to psychoanalysis and other styles of therapy popular at the time, in this approach, the focus of therapeutic conversations was not on problems and trying to understand their possible past causes, but on goals; on what the client wanted their future to be like and how the therapist, through good and empowering questions, could help them find ways to move forward. "The client knows the solution to their problem; they just don't know that they know it" was one of the philosophical premises of solution-focused psychology.

The skills approach presented in this book is founded on the principles of solution-focused psychology. The aim is not to dwell on the causes and background of challenges, but to explore and discover ways to help children move on with the support of the important people in their life.

interest. Today, the Kids'Skills method is being used by a wide range of professionals in many countries around the world. Books describing the method have been published in more than 20 languages.

We developed the Kids'Skills method originally as a tool for teachers and other people who work with children, but because the approach is so simple, safe, and easy to learn, parents, grandparents and other people participating in raising children can utilise it also. The method was borne in a group where the children were 5–6 years old, but it soon became evident that the very same steps and principles could be used with older children too. In fact, the approach is blind to age. With slight adjustments, it is suitable for human beings of all ages.

Skills thinking, the backbone of Kids'Skills, is founded on the idea that no matter what the child's challenge or difficulty is, you don't focus on the difficulty, but instead you focus on the skill the child needs to learn for the difficulty to pass. Children usually become uneasy when we try to talk with them about their problems or difficulties, but they quite enjoy talking about skills – not only skills that they have already acquired, but also skills they can see that they would benefit from getting better at.

Skills thinking calls for seeing children through a different lens. It requires us to see beyond problems and to figure out what skill the child needs to become better at to conquer his or her challenge. To do that, to figure out what skill the child needs to improve, is, however, easier said than done. My intention in this book is to help you discover how you can convert not only small everyday challenges, but also more serious problems, into skills that your child can learn, and how you can support your child in acquiring those skills.

Let's start with a story told by a woman who had participated in a Kids'Skills training program, and as part of her training wrote a report of how she had used the method to help her 6-year-old goddaughter conquer a challenge. I think the story is one of many charming examples of how the skills approach can be applied in practice.

Jasmin, 6-year-old girl

Jasmin had several challenges. She had challenges with dressing herself, going to the toilet, and going to bed. When she was supposed to get dressed in the mornings, she refused to put on the clothes her mother had chosen for her. All clothes felt uncomfortable for her. She only wanted to use the same old worn-out clothes. She abhorred all winter clothes, rainy season clothes, mittens, and hats. Going to bed in the evening was difficult for her. She demanded to stay up as late as her parents, and this led to a mighty struggle almost every evening. The third challenge was that Jasmin refused to wipe her bottom after defecating in the toilet and always required an adult to assist her. In kindergarten, Jasmin refused to defecate all day, with the result that she often suffered from tummy aches in the evenings.

Jasmin's godmother, Emma, who had taken some training in the skills approach, offered to help Jasmin's worried parents. When they all sat together, the conversation first revolved around various skills that Jasmin had already acquired and that she was good at. For example, Jasmin already knew how to read and write even if she was not attending school yet (in her country, school starts officially when children are 7). She also knew how to swim and how to ride a bicycle. Jasmin appeared proud as everyone talked about her many skills.

Soon the topic of the conversation shifted from skills she already had to skills she needed to learn next. The parents' wish-list consisted of 3 skills. They were – as one might guess – "putting on clothes skill," "going to sleep skill," and "toilet skill." The parents discussed the various benefits of all the 3 skills and Emma suggested casually that, when Jasmin learned one of the 3 skills, a celebration could be arranged in her honour if she wanted it. Of the 3 options, Jasmin chose the 'toilet skill.' Jasmin decided to call her skill "the wiping skill"

"What good would it do you to learn to wipe your bottom yourself?" Emma asked. Jasmin wasn't able to give an answer, but she volunteered that she dreaded that her hand would be tarnished with faeces. That explained, at least partially, why Jasmin had not been keen on learning to wipe her behind by herself. Her parents explained that the wiping skill was important because then Jasmin wouldn't have tummy aches in the evenings, she wouldn't need to sit on the toilet waiting for someone to come and help her, and next year, when she entered school, she would be expected to be able to do it herself. Jasmin listened attentively. It was then agreed that the parents would help Jasmin start practising her skill at home. Her mother promised to be by her side, advising her on how to wipe herself and also how to wash her hands in case she would accidentally tarnish her hands. Jasmin herself suggested that she would start by wiping only once while her mother would wipe the rest.

"Can you think of some creature that can support you in learning the wiping skill?" Emma asked. Jasmin said that she wanted her helper to be Super Furball (a smart animated guinea pig). Super Furball had helped her before when, some time ago, she had to get a vaccination at a visit to the health nurse. Jasmin wanted to place a picture of the Super Furball in the toilet to remind her of her skill.

Emma brought up the celebration again. "When you have learned the wiping skill," she said, "We can bake together and have a party if you want." Jasmin found the idea appealing and this led to a discussion about who would be invited and what kind of cake would be served at the party.

One week later, when Emma talked with Jasmin's mother on the phone, she found out that Jasmin had gotten well on the way with practising her skill. The first few days, Jasmin's mother had guided Jasmin, but after that she had managed to complete the wiping herself. Every time she had done it by herself, her mother had given her a Super Furball sticker, which was pasted into a notebook reserved for the purpose. The parents had made an agreement with Jasmin that once she had collected 10 stickers, it would be time to arrange the party. She had already made so much progress that she had given her mother permission to tell the kindergarten teachers about the skill, which made it possible for the staff in kindergarten to support her in learning her skill there, too.

There were also some setbacks. One day, when she had not yet collected more than 6 stickers, Jasmin suddenly called her mother from the toilet to come wipe her.

"Why did you call me? Have you forgotten your skills?" her mother asked.

"No, I haven't," Jasmin said, "I can do it. I have even done it in kindergarten."

"Ok, show me how good you can do it," said her mother.

Jasmin refused to show her mother her skill and complained that her stool was so loose that she didn't want to wipe at all.

"It's not the end of the world, honey," her mother said. "Let's do this. You wipe once and I wipe the rest." Jasmin agreed to her mother's proposal but ended up wiping all the way by herself anyway. Her mother pasted a sticker into the notebook and later that day they called Emma to tell her what had happened.

When there were 10 stickers in the notebook, Jasmin designed a card together with her mother to invite Emma to the party. The party was an enjoyable event with cake and other delicacies served. After everyone had had some cake, Emma suggested to Jasmin to cut out hearts from cardboard to give to people who had helped and supported her. Jasmin cut out several hearts and gave one to each of her parents, one to Emma, and one to the kindergarten teachers.

"What skill will you go for next now that you've already mastered the wiping skill so well?" Emma asked Jasmin.

"My next skill is the modelling skill," Jasmin replied.

"Modelling skill? What skill is that?" Emma wanted to know.

It turned out that Jasmin had been playing a game with her parents that they had called "modelling game." It was a game where Jasmin played a model who presented various new clothes to her parents and simultaneously practised getting accustomed to wearing diverse clothes.

Children participate actively,

others support them.

The manner in which Emma partnered with Jasmin's parents to help Jasmin overcome one of her challenges exemplifies the skills approach: Instead of talking about problems, the focus was on skills to learn. The child was an active participant in all steps of the process, and all the important people in the child's life were supporting and helping the child to acquire the skill.

* * *

Photo by mali desha on Unsplash

3

HOW TO CONVERT CHALLENGES INTO SKILLS TO LEARN

The word 'skill' means that the child can handle

a given challenging situation in the desired manner.

DOI: 10.4324/9781003435723-3

The skills approach – or the idea of helping children overcome challenges by learning skills – has some significant benefits. First, the concept of "skill" conveys the idea of hope. We all associate skills with "learning," which is another word that generates hope. When we focus on talking about skills and learning, we inevitably conjure up an atmosphere of hope for change.

Second, skills thinking fosters collaboration with children. Your child is more likely to collaborate with you when you talk with them about skills they have already learned and skills they might benefit from learning rather than about their problems and difficulties.

Third, the skills approach makes it easier for you to collaborate with the other adults involved in caring for your child. If you focus on the child's problems and difficulties in your conversations with them, they often respond by starting to tell you what they think is causing your child's problems. Such speculations are often unhelpful and can contribute to despair rather than hope. The skills approach helps you to escape this pitfall. When the focus is on skills to learn, your fellow carers will find it easier to support you in helping your child learn whatever skill he or she needs to learn.

Converting challenges into skills is easier said than done

A prerequisite of skills thinking is converting children's problems into skills that they can learn. This is easier said than done. The idea is simple, but in real life it is not always easy to figure out what skill the child needs to learn to overcome his or her problem.

I have often heard people say that the idea of skills thinking is all well and good, but putting it into practice is much more difficult than one might think at first. "I know exactly what problem the child has," a teacher once said to me, "but I find it difficult to figure out what skill the child needs to become better at for the problem to pass."

Converting challenges into learnable skills – what I have sometimes called "skilling" – requires creative thinking. The premise is, that regardless of what the child's challenge happens to be, there is always a skill to be discovered that, if mastered, will eliminate the problem, or at least reduce its intensity.

A German psychologist friend of mine, who also teaches solution-focused therapy and coaching like myself, once said to me: "Our students like the skills approach a lot, but they often find it difficult to figure out what skill the child should learn to overcome a particular problem. You should write a dictionary in which the reader can look up all the common problems that children have and then see what skill the child needs to learn to overcome that particular problem."

"I understand what you are saying," I objected, "but it's not possible. From knowing what the child's problem is, you cannot directly draw a line to a particular skill the child would need to learn to overcome the problem. To figure out what would be a relevant skill for the child to learn requires us to have a conversation with the child, and perhaps also with the other adults who are involved in caring for the child."

"Yes, yes, I know," my colleague said, shrugging his shoulders, "but anyway, people would need some instructions on how to convert problems into skills."

Following my colleague's advice, I present next some general ideas of how to convert problems into skills that children can learn.

A better way to handle a challenging situation

When I help parents convert their child's challenge into a skill, I often start by asking them what situations their child finds challenging. Once I have heard some examples of such situations, I can invite the parents to think about how they would want their child to learn to respond in a better way in those situations. Here's an example of how I would attempt to help a parent to shift from challenges to skills.

Mother: They have complained about my daughter's behaviour at kindergarten. She apparently hits the other children there.

Me: Do you know in what situations it happens? What situations are difficult for her to handle?

Mother: They say it happens when she wants to play with a toy that another child is playing with.

Me: What does she do?

Mother: She tries to grab the toy and when the other child refuses to give it to her, she becomes frustrated and that's when the hitting happens.

Me: How would you want her to learn to handle those situations instead?

Mother: In a more mature way.

Me: Sure, and what would you want her to learn to do instead?

Mother: I would like her to learn to ask kindly if she can have the toy and then, if the other child refuses, I would want her to be able to take "no" for an answer.

Me: What would you want her to learn to say that would tell you that she has learned to take "no" for an answer?

Mother: I would want her to say something like, "Can I have it when you don't want to play with it anymore?"

Me: Ok, so that's the skill you would want your daughter to learn.

In other words, to figure out what skill you want your child to learn, think about how your child tends to respond in situations that are difficult for him or her to deal with, and ask yourself how you would want your child to learn to handle similar situations in the future.

A skill describes desired behaviour

An important thing to keep in mind when we talk about skills is that "skill" does not mean stopping undesired behaviour. It means learning to behave in a more desirable manner.

It is difficult for children to stop – or reduce – undesired behaviour. For example, if you want your child to learn not to shout out in class, the skill for your child to learn should not be stated as: "I will refrain from shouting out in class," but as: "I can raise my hand to talk in class and wait for permission to talk," or if you want your child to learn to avoid getting into fights with other children, the skill for your child to learn should not be stated as "I will not pick fights with other children," but as "I will learn to walk away from situations in which I get cross with other children." The skill to learn should always point to a description of the desired behaviour rather than to a description of the undesired behaviour.

Skill is not the ability to refrain from acting in the wrong way.

It is the ability to act in the right way.

Sometimes when I have given talks to parents about the skills approach, I have claimed tongue-in-cheek:

> "Did you know that there is a filter in children's auditive nerve, the nerve that carries nerve impulses from the ear to the brain? That filter effectively removes words such as 'don't' and 'stop' from sentences. If you say to your son: 'I'm telling you again, Dan, *don't* shout at me,' Dan will hear you saying: 'I'm telling you again, Dan, shout at me.' Or if you say to your daughter: 'Julia, I told you to stop that. I don't like you fiddling with your food,' she will hear you saying: 'Julia, I told you that I like you fiddling with your food.'"

By saying so, I'm jokingly making the point that children often fail to follow parents' instructions if the instruction contains denial-words, such as "don't," "stop," or "not." This is not because they are just stubborn or pig-headed, but rather because their brains are not mature enough to handle instructions lacking clues about what to do instead.

For this reason, parenting guides often recommend that when giving instructions to our children, we should try to tell them what we want them to do rather than only telling them what not to do. Here are a few examples of converting don't-do-instructions into do-instructions:

Don't shout	→	Speak softly!
Don't beg	→	Ask nicely!
Don't run	→	Walk!
Don't play with your food	→	Eat neatly!

I once gave an evening lecture for parents at a kindergarten where I talked about converting don't-do-instructions to do-instructions. There were some parents present who had not succeeded in finding a babysitter for the evening and who therefore had brought their child along to the event. A few days after the event, one of the mothers who had been in the audience that evening with her son related to the kindergarten teacher the following incident. She had heard her own son running with some other children and making noise in the hallway of their apartment house. There had been complaints about the children's noise before, so the mother opened the door and shouted to the children, "No running in the hallway!" Her son quickly responded to her saying, "Mom, you're not supposed to say, "Don't run." You should say, "Walk." "I think my son got the idea from the evening lecture better than I did," the mom said with a smile on her face.

The idea of replacing don't-do-instructions with do-instructions may seem simple, but in real-life situations it is often very difficult to think of how to instruct a child without using words such as "stop," "don't" or "no." I am reminded of a personal experience from years ago when one of my two daughters was around 7 years old.

I was driving the car returning home from shopping and my daughter was sitting in the back seat with her friend. I felt an awkward annoying movement in my backside, and it took a moment for me to realize that it was my daughter behind me kicking the back of my seat with her feet.

"Stop that kicking," I told her. It didn't help. The kicking continued as if I hadn't said anything. I figured I need to intensify my message, so I said something along the lines of, "Stop that kicking immediately. Don't you understand, it disturbs my driving? You don't want us to end up in an accident, do you?" Instead of my well-chosen words having had an influence on her, the two girls started to giggle in the back seat. They apparently thought that I was being funny. Finally, I couldn't think of anything else to say, so I probably said something to the effect of, "If you don't stop kicking, I will stop the car and both of you will walk all the way back home." My threat did not do the trick, judging by the fact that the giggling only intensified in the back seat. I asked myself how to approach the situation using skills thinking. Would it be possible to handle the situation by rewarding her for desirable behaviour rather than threatening her with consequences if she didn't stop her undesirable behaviour? I didn't have a clue as to what to say, so I said what first came to mind: "It would be easier for me to concentrate on driving, so if you keep your feet to yourself, I'm prepared to pay you 10 cents for each time you don't kick my seat." The words that had come out of my mouth sounded weird to me, but to my surprise the kicking ended, and the back seat became quiet. I soon forgot about the incident but later that same day, when I was putting her to bed, she suddenly extended her arm towards me. "What?" I asked her. "Give me 80 cents," she said. "You owe me that amount. You promised me in the car that you would pay me 10 cents for each time I didn't kick you, and I counted."

I don't recall if my daughter ever got that 80 cents from me that she felt she had earned by refraining eight times from kicking me, but the incident made me think. Most people these days agree that praising or rewarding children for good behaviour is a more effective way of influencing them than reprimanding them for bad behaviour, but practising this principle in real life is not easy. It simply wouldn't work if our children started to expect us to reward them every time they didn't do something they shouldn't do.

To complicate matters, as parents we are not usually content with our children simply following instructions. We want more; we want them to learn to follow our instructions without us having to repeat our instructions to them over and over again. But how on earth are we supposed to get our children to turn our instructions into habits so that they will do what we expect from them unprompted? Perhaps we should think of that as a skill too. Being able to do something unprompted is, in and of itself, a skill that children can learn and become better at. Allow me to share the personal experience of an attempt to deal with this challenge.

My daughter was around 6 when I told her: "Darling, I would like you to learn to place your dishes into the dishwasher after you have finished eating. I have noticed that you do it when I tell you to do it, but I would like you to learn to do it spontaneously, without me having to tell you to do it." I noticed that she was listening to me, so I continued, "Let's do this from now on. I will continue to remind you to take your dishes to the dishwasher, but when I remind you, don't do it immediately. Wait a minute or two, perhaps you can count to ten, and then, after that, take your dishes to the dishwasher spontaneously as if I hadn't said anything. Shall we try?" I thought that my daughter might find my suggestion foolish, but she decided to play along. I reminded her of what she needed to do. She waited for a while and then "spontaneously" took her dishes and placed them into the dishwasher. My daughter's initiative grew over time, and I like to think that our foolish little game contributed to that positive development.

Search for exceptions to the rule

Here's another practical way that can help you figure out a skill for your child to learn. For example, if the rule is that your child is glued to the smart phone, then any exceptions to that rule – that is, times when he or she puts the smart phone away to do something else – can give a clue as to the skill he or she might need to learn to reduce the problem.

Consider the following example in which a parent uses the exceptions approach to help the child figure out what skill he or she needs to learn to avoid getting into arguments with teachers at school.

Parent: *What could you do to avoid getting into all those arguments with your teachers?*

Child: *I don't know.*

Parent: *There must be some teachers you get along with better than others, aren't there?*

Child: *I get along fine with my PE teacher.*

Parent:	*How do you explain that? What is that you do differently that makes you get along with your PE teacher?*
Child:	*I never talk back to my PE teacher.*
Parent:	*You don't? What do you do instead?*
Child:	*I pretend to listen. I nod and say, "Ok."*
Parent:	*So, you found something that works with your PE teacher. What do you call that skill?*
Child:	*I don't know. Good behaviour, I guess.*
Parent:	*Good behaviour. Ok, so you already seem to possess that skill. You can do it with your PE teacher. Do you think it would be a good thing if you started to use that skill of yours with the other teachers too?*

Identify the opposite of the problem

Too much analysis can cause paralysis.

When parents or teachers are concerned about a child's behaviour, they often use problem language and problem words to talk about what they are worried about. They may say, for example, that the child is "impulsive," has "low self-esteem," or "lacks empathy." Such sweeping problem descriptions don't tell us much about what the child's actual challenges are, but if you can think of what the opposite of the problem description is, it becomes easier to figure out what skill the child might benefit from learning. The following dialogue would be an example of how such a conversation might look.

Parent:	*My son is extremely shy.*
Me:	*You would want him to be less shy?*
Parent:	*Yes. I think he suffers from his shyness.*
Me:	*Hmm. Not shy. What do you call a child who is not shy?*
Parent:	*I don't know, maybe "brave," or "socially brave."*
Me:	*That makes sense. I guess children are always somewhere on the continuum from shy to socially brave. I wonder, what do you think would be the first small sign for you that your son is making progress towards becoming socially braver?*

Parent:	He would not hide in his room when we have guests coming over.
Me:	I see. What would he be doing instead?
Parent:	He would open his door, and at least greet the guests.
Me:	Would that be a skill you'd want him to learn? Would you be less worried about him if he managed to learn that skill?
Parent:	We would both, me and my wife, be very much relieved if he learned to do that.

Shift focus from explanations to behaviour

Sometimes when parents, teachers, and other caretakers talk about children's problems, they speak in a way that contains scarce information about the child's challenges, but plenty of information of their ideas of the underlying causes of the child's challenges. For example, a teacher might say that a child lacks empathy, that a child is traumatized, or that a child has low self-esteem. Such grand words are not descriptions of the child's challenges, but explanations of the possible causes of the child's challenges.

To identify skills for children to learn, it may be useful to temporarily set aside our explanations and focus instead on what it is that the child finds challenging, and then to figure out, based on that information, what skill the child might benefit from learning. The following dialogue is an example how such a conversation might look.

Parent:	My son annoys everyone with his egoistic and attention-seeking behaviour.
Me:	What does he do that makes you think that his behaviour is egoistic and attention-seeking?
Parent:	One thing that he does a lot is interrupting other people. When a thought pops up in his mind, he blurts it out without letting other people complete their sentences.
Me:	Would you say that the habit of interrupting other people is one of his challenges?
Parent:	Yes, that's definitely one of them.
Me:	I understand. Could it be something to start with?

Parent:	Maybe.
Me:	What would you say he needs to learn to do to avoid interrupting others?
Parent:	He needs to learn to be more patient. He needs to learn to wait and let the other person finish talking.
Me:	That's an important skill for children to learn. Do you have any idea of what he could do to be able to do that?
Parent:	I sometimes secretly cross my fingers to tell myself to listen patiently when my customers explain to me things that I am not all that interested in hearing. Perhaps he should learn to do something similar.
Me:	Listening is not an easy skill for children to learn, but if he agrees to try to become better at it, he might at least make some progress.

* * *

To apply the skills approach in parenting starts with converting our wishes into skills that children can learn, but that is just the first step on the way. You will obviously also need to figure out how to get your child interested in learning and motivated to make the effort to learn that skill.

In the next chapter I will present to you a wide range of ways that the skills approach can help motivate children to learn the skills we believe they would benefit from learning.

4

HOW TO MOTIVATE CHILDREN TO LEARN SKILLS

If a child wants to learn something,
they will learn it.

DOI: 10.4324/9781003435723-4

When speaking about the skills approach to parents or educators, I find that my audiences often struggle with two questions. First, how to figure out which skill(s) the child needs to learn to overcome their problem and second, how to motivate the child to learn that skill. In this chapter, I will assume that you already have an idea of what skill you think your child would benefit from learning, and that you are now interested in discovering how to motivate him or her to learn that skill.

Below I propose to you 15 approaches to motivating your child to develop a skill, approaches that are consistent with the skills mindset presented in this book. I hope you find them useful as you strive to help your child to learn important skills for life.

1. Start by talking with your child about skills that they have already learned

Before you propose that your child learn a new skill, talk with them about the many skills they have already acquired. "Honey, you have already learned so many skills. You have learned to snowboard, you have learned to speak a bit of Spanish, and you have even learned to be nicer to your baby sister. You are good at learning whatever you decide to learn." By making sure that your child feels proud of the skills that they have developed or managed to improve, you increase the likelihood that your child will be willing to talk with you about potential skills that they would benefit from learning next.

2. Use "we" instead of "I" messages

When you propose a skill for your child to learn, say "we" instead of "I" whenever possible. For example, "We think it would be good for you to learn..." rather than "I think it would be good for you to learn..." Children are more likely to abide by your wish if they understand that it is not only you who thinks the skill is important, but something that everyone else who cares about them would also want them to learn or become better at.

3. Find out what skill your child wants to learn

If your child shows no interest in learning the skill that you would like them to learn, don't worry. Instead, ask your child if they can think of some other skill that they would benefit from learning and that they would rather master. By inviting your child to start by learning a skill of their own choosing, you provide them with a positive learning experience, which in turn will prepare the child for learning further skills.

4. Discuss the benefits of learning the skill with your child

To be motivated to learn any skill, your child needs to see that there are some benefits of doing so. Therefore, I advise having a conversation with your child about the advantages of mastering the skill not only to your child, but also to various important people in your child's life.

Too often, when parents and educators try to convince children of the benefits of learning a particular skill, they often do it by pointing out the many negative consequences and problems that the child will escape by learning it. A better motivational strategy is to help the child become aware of the positive consequences, or benefits, of learning the skill. For example, rather than saying something like, "If you learn to be quiet during lessons, your teacher will no longer scold you," consider saying something along the lines of, "If you learn to be quiet during lessons, you will earn the respect of your teacher." Or instead of saying, "If you learn to be cool in the supermarket even if I don't buy you the things you want, then I will not have to be ashamed of you," you might begin your sentence in the same way but conclude with: "...then we will all be proud of you."

When discussing the benefits of learning a particular skill with a child, it is also important for the child to feel that the benefits you are talking about are relevant and meaningful to them. For example, if your child is passionate about football, it would make sense to talk with them about how learning a particular skill will help them to become a better football player, or if friendships are extremely important to your child, it would make sense to talk with them about how the skill you would like them to learn will help them improve their relationships with their friends.

5. Join your child in learning new skills

You can reinforce your child's willingness to learn skills by deciding to learn some skill of your own simultaneously. It is easier for your child to say yes to the proposal to learn a skill if you, and possibly other family members as well, are also learning some skills. I am reminded of a 10-year-old boy who was supposed to learn the skill of finishing his homework in time. He told his mother, "Mom, you also need to learn a skill. You yell at me. You need to learn to talk softly to me." The mother's decision to learn the skill of "not yelling", or better, expressing her wishes in a gentle way to her son, added to the son's motivation to learn the skill that she wanted him to learn.

6. Reinforce your child's self-confidence

Another useful motivational tool is to tell your child that you are convinced that they will be able to learn the skill you want them to learn, and to explain to them what makes you think so. You may say, "I am sure you can do it," and then continue by saying something like, "because you are so good at learning new things," or "because you clearly understand why getting better at it will be good for you," or "because we will all help and support you," or "because you have already made some progress," or "because you are so persistent that if you decide to learn something, you certainly will."

7. Make sure the skill is not too big

Your child may back off if you propose they learn a skill that appears too difficult. It is important to divide challenging skills into smaller, or incremental, skills that seem possible for the child to learn easily. For example, if your daughter suffers from selective mutism, or the fear of talking to anyone beyond the nuclear family, you can help her by starting with baby steps. You may engage her in a conversation with a hand-puppet that impersonates her teacher, or help her to answer her teacher's or her classmate's chat message on the school's online message board.

8. Ask your child to give a name to the skill

Encourage your child to give a name to the skill you want them to learn. Children are more motivated to learn skills if they get to decide what their skill is to be called. In addition, a good name for the skill helps to stimulate the child's creativity. The child's creativity is an important building block in figuring out what the child can do to practice and improve the skill and how other people can best support them in their learning process.

9. Ask your child to appoint supporters

Children need other people's support to learn new skills. They will benefit from all the help and encouragement they can get. Having a team of supporters adds to their optimism, which in turn boosts their motivation. So, invite your child to think about which people to ask to be their supporters. You or other family members are an obvious choice. Other children, particularly if they are a few years older than your child and your child looks up to them, also make good supporters.

The supporters can help your child in many ways. They can, for example:

- help your child understand why it pays to learn the skill,
- admire your child when your child masters the skill,

- offer ideas about how to practise the skill,
- remind your child of the skill if your child sometimes forgets it,
- join a celebration at which your child is acknowledged for having learned the skill.

10. Encourage your child to have an imaginary supporter, too

Suggest that your child choose or invent an animal, creature, or superhero that will support them in learning the skill. Once they have chosen their imaginary supporter – say, a Pokémon character – don't hesitate to ask your child, "How will the Pokémon help you?" You may be surprised at how creative your child is at inventing ways in which their imaginary supporter can help them and motivate them to learn their skill.

11. Plan to celebrate learning the skill

For many children, the idea that there will be a celebration when they have learned their skill is a powerful motivator. Bring up the possibility of such a celebration well in advance and allow your child to have some say in how such a celebration should look, where it should take place, who should be invited, and what should happen during the event. The idea of celebrating learning may seem like just another way of rewarding the child, but I prefer to think of it as an important step in the process of growth: honouring the child for their accomplishment and thanking the child's supporters for their help and encouragement.

12. Help your child come up with a fun way to practise the skill

To learn any skill, children need to practise. This is a challenge since children are not automatically motivated to practise their skills. Therefore, it is important to invent fun and rewarding ways for the child to practise the skill, ways that add to the child's motivation to master it.

Would it be possible to turn learning the skill into a game that your child finds motivating? For example, small children are often highly motivated to show how good they already are at performing their skill. Showing how good you already are is more rewarding and fun to the child than practising the skill, but from the point of view of learning, showing counts as practising.

Consider asking your child what they would want to do to acquire their skill. "What can you do to learn your skill?", "How can you practice your skill?", "How will you remember your skill?" Your child may surprise you by coming up with creative ideas for developing their skills. Another possibility is to find a way to use your smartphone to make learning more interesting and rewarding to your child. "Show me your skill and I'll shoot a TikTok video of you doing it!"

In the case of younger children, you may want to find a way to involve a puppet or a cuddly toy in the learning process. "Look at this hippo. Can you see, his diaper is wet? I think he is old enough to learn to wee in the toilet. Let's help the hippo learn to wee in the toilet. What shall we do to help him learn to do that?"

13. Discover diverse ways to praise your child

Ask your child how they want you to show your appreciation when they manage their skill. Some children respond positively to direct verbal praise, while others prefer to be acknowledged with a gesture or some other inconspicuous signal. Invite your child to participate in working out a unique and age-appropriate way to praise them that fits their personality.

14. Find a way to remind your child of the skill

Children do not acquire skills overnight, even when they are committed to learning them. Sooner or later, they are bound to experience setbacks or instances when they forget the skill they are learning and fall temporarily back on their previous pattern of behavior. Instead of calling such incidents "setbacks," though, it may be better to think of them simply as moments of forgetting their skill.

Children are sensitive to the way in which you remind them of the skill they are in the process of learning. Reminding them of their skill in a way that makes them feel criticised tends to have a negative effect on their motivation while reminding them in a gentler and mutually agreed-upon manner can help enhance their motivation.

Try to find a way of responding to "forgetting the skill" that fits with the skills mindset. Ask your child what they would want you – and other people – to do to help them remember their skill: "How do you want me to remind you of your skill when you sometimes forget it?"

15. Offer your child an opportunity to help someone else learn the skill they have learned

You can tell your child, "When you have learned your skill, you can help someone else, maybe another child in your class, to learn the same skill." Children take satisfaction in teaching skills that they have acquired to other people. The mere idea of teaching their skill to others in the future is reinforcing and serves as an additional incentive for your child to want to learn the skill they will benefit from learning.

* * *

Now that you not only have an idea of how to convert children's problems into skills they can learn, but you are also familiar with a wide range of means to motivate your child to learn a skill he or she has agreed to learn, let's move on to talking about how you might apply skills thinking in your day-to-day life with your children.

5

HOW TO USE
THE SKILLS APPROACH
IN DAY-TO-DAY PARENTING

Show your child that you have faith in them,
and they will have faith in themself.

DOI: 10.4324/9781003435723-5

The skills approach was originally developed as a method for teachers and other people working with children to help them overcome challenges, but the approach is equally well-suited for supporting children's growth in the everyday life of families, even when children are not presently struggling with any challenges that they would need to overcome.

If you want to use skills thinking in your day-to-day life with your child, I recommend that you start by attaching a poster (see poster adjacent page) to your refrigerator door to remind yourself of the following key steps of the approach.

Step 1. Think of your wishes as skills for your child to learn

I assume that by reading the previous chapters of this book, you have become quite familiar with the idea that all sorts of children's challenges can be viewed as skills that they haven't learned yet. Imagine that you are wearing a pair of spectacles that allow you to see your child in a different light; not as a child who is struggling with challenges, but as a child who needs support and help in developing skills needed to deal with various challenging situations that he or she is confronted with in life.

Step 2. Explain to your child why the skill is an important one to learn

If you want your child to learn a skill, prepare to have a conversation with him or her about why it is important to learn such a skill.

When I teach this principle in my lectures, I often illustrate the idea by showing the audience a YouTube clip in which you can see a German father having a conversation with his 6-year-old son about homework. In the video, we can see the boy is sitting at a table with his father writing the letters of the alphabet into his notebook.

Think of your wishes as skills for your child to learn

Shy away from criticising your child for acting in the wrong way and think, instead, about what you would want your child to learn to do or say in similar situations. Think of the preferred way of responding as a skill that your child can learn with the support of other people.

Explain to your child why the skill is an important one to learn

Your child may not understand why you want them to learn a particular skill. Help your child see why it is important and beneficial for them to learn the skill.

Build your child's confidence

Encourage your child by letting them know why you have faith that they will be able to succeed in learning the skill.

Remind your child in an agreeable manner

Make an agreement with your child about how you will remind them of the skill when needed in a kind way that does not undermine their willingness to learn the skill.

Reinforce your child's learning

Reinforce your child's learning by ensuring that they have opportunities to feel proud of their successes and progress.

"I don't see why I have to do this," the boy complains to his father with a desperate look on his face.

"Say it again," says the father. "I didn't quite understand what you said."

"When I grow up, I will be a truck driver or an excavator operator," the boy answers.

"So what?"

"If I drive a truck or I operate an excavator, then in that work I will not need to write anything."

"You won't?" the father ponders aloud, "But you will at least have to be able to calculate. If you operate an excavator, you will need to calculate how high the wall you build and how deep the hole you dig needs to be. If you drive a truck you will need to calculate how heavy your load can be, and how long your braking distance is depending on the speed you are driving. All those are things that you will need to be able to calculate."

"Yes, but I don't intend to be any kind of master builder. I will just be operating the excavator and driving trucks. I will not be doing any of the other jobs."

"Yes, yes, but you will need a driver's licence. And if you want to have a driver's licence, you will need to be able to read. You have to pass the written exam, which is required. There you need to provide answers to questions that you will need to read and understand."

The boy listens to his father's justifications with a serious and thoughtful look on his face. Then he takes a deep sigh, moves the hand in which he is holding his pen back onto the page of his notepad and continues with his task of drawing the letters of the alphabet.

In the video, the boy's father succeeded in convincing his son of the importance of learning the skill with just a few well-chosen words. He justified the importance of the skill from within his son's own perspective; he helped his son to see that the skill of reading and writing would help him achieve his own goals. If your child dreams about becoming a dancer, consider justifying the skill you want them to learn by helping them realize how the skill will help them to succeed as a dancer. Likewise, if your child dreams about becoming a football champion, consider using justifications that allow the child to see how the skill you would want them to learn can help them be more successful in football.

The following personal experience of mine is another illustration of the same idea.

When one of my two daughters was 5 years old, I sat in her room one evening with a pile of papers by her bed as she was ready to go to sleep.

"What are you doing, Dad?" she asked me.

I was not supposed to start having a conversation with her as it was her sleepy time, but for some reason I ended up answering her: "I am working on a book about how to help children overcome problems," I said.

"Oh, I don't have any problems," she responded.

"Well, the book is not really about how to help children overcome problems, but about how to help them learn skills," I explained.

"Oh, but I also don't have any skills that I would need to learn," she said.

"Everyone has skills that they need to become better at. You too."

"What skill do I need to learn?"

"For example, you need to learn to go to sleep without always having that bright light shining right into your face. You should learn to go to sleep in the dark, or with just a small night lamp giving a dim light in the room."

"Why?" she asked. She demanded to hear a justification as if she had been familiar with the idea that we need to explain to children why we want them to learn a particular skill.

"Well, for one thing, because you like to invite friends for sleepovers and it would be easier for you to invite your friends for sleepovers if their parents knew that you have learned to go to sleep with just a small night lamp on. Your bright light keeps you and your friends awake sometimes for hours."

I noticed that my daughter was listening to me, so I couldn't resist the temptation to continue: "And besides that, you would probably also get more sleep-over invitations if your friends' parents found out that you have learned to go to sleep in dim light." My daughter appeared thoughtful. "And we would even save some electricity," I added. I was surprised by what happened next. My daughter extended her arm and pressed the switch button to turn off the bright reading light that had been shining in her face.

It's better to praise children for their desired behaviour
Than to scold them for their undesired behaviour

Many parents have the bad habit that when their children act in an undesirable manner, they start presenting why-questions to the child, such as: "Why do you have to keep talking all the time?" "Why did you grab that toy from that boy's hand?" "Why are you being so slow?" "Why don't you eat your food?" "Why are you talking back to me?"

The problem with such why-questions is that children are unable to provide an answer. They don't know why they do what they do, and they experience why-questions as a form of scolding criticism rather than as genuine questions. Therefore, it is not surprising that children often respond to their parents' why-questions with shrugging their shoulders and saying, "I don't know." Another problem with why-questions is that they trigger children to fabricate excuses for their behaviour, putting the blame on someone else: "Because you are so stupid!" "Because everyone else is doing it too," "Because Janet bullies me," "Because I am angry for you not letting me have my smartphone."

Why-questions may sometimes be outright harmful. The child may not be able to come up with an answer, but he or she may still start to silently wonder about the reasons for his or her behaviour. There is a risk that as the child does the thinking, he or she comes up with a conclusion that there is something fundamentally wrong about him or her, that he or she is in some way deviant or flawed. Such conclusions undermine the child's self-confidence and reduce his or her faith in being able to learn to behave differently.

Put more emphasis on figuring out
why it pays to act in the desired way
than on figuring out why your child
acts in the undesired way.

One method that I recommend to parents who want to stop asking their children why-questions is to replace explanation-seeking why-questions with skills-focused why-questions. Skills-focused why-questions do not seek to find answers to why the child is acting in an undesirable manner. They seek to find answers to why it would be profitable for the child to learn to behave in a better or more desirable manner.

> "Larry, it's time for you to learn to sleep in your own bed throughout the night. Do you know why it is important for big boys to learn to sleep in their own bed?"

> "Jesse, I want you to learn to talk nicely to your mom. It's not nice of you to speak rudely to her. Do you know why it is important for all children to learn to talk nicely to their mothers?"

> "I have talked with your father about how much daily screen-time we are willing to give you at your age. It is important to us that you don't spend too much time on your phone and that you also do other things. Do you know why that is so important to us? Do you understand why we are concerned about it?"

Explaining to your child, in a way that your child can understand, why you want him or her to learn a particular skill, is an important first step in getting him or her initially interested in learning the skill, but this alone is not sufficient to do the trick. No matter how well you succeed in convincing your child of the benefits of the skill, you will need to take additional measures to ensure that your child is sufficiently motivated to make the effort of learning the skill.

Step 3. Build your child's confidence

In the olden days, it was not uncommon for some parents to try to boost their child's learning by criticising them. They might say to their child things like:

- You can't do it.
- That won't work.
- How can it be so difficult?
- Your sister learned much faster.
- Try, at least.

- You don't even try.
- Oh no, let me show you how to do it.
- What's taking so long?
- Is it really that difficult?

Parents who speak to their children in this way probably hope that their critical words would work to increase their child's motivation by triggering in the child a desire to prove the parents wrong.

Criticising children does not, however, usually boost their self-confidence. It is a risky approach to parenting. If children internalise their parents' critical comments, their self-confidence can suffer serious damage.

Contemporary ideas about parenting rely more on encouragement and praise than on criticism and fault finding. If you wish to boost your child's motivation to learn, it is better to avoid criticism or focusing on failures. Boost the child's confidence instead; convince your child that even if you are fully aware of how difficult it can be to develop new skills, nevertheless, you – and also other people – are convinced that he or she will be able to make it. You might say, for example:

- You can do it.
- You can learn anything.
- You are good at learning things.
- You are a fast learner.
- You can learn anything you put your mind to.
- You didn't succeed yet, but it was a good try.
- I could see that you tried your best.
- You have already done it many times.
- You have already started to learn.
- You have learned more difficult things.
- You will learn because you know that it is important.
- You will learn because you are my child.
- You will learn because we will all help you.
- You will learn because I know you want to learn.

Your child's confidence – the child's faith in being able to learn a skill – is influenced by how strongly the people around the child believe that he or she can do it. The more people express their confidence in the child, the more likely it is that the child also becomes optimistic about learning the skill.

Step 4. Remind your child in an agreeable manner

Finding a good way to remind the child of the skill when needed is an important element of skills thinking. The recommendation is that you reserve some time to make an agreement with your child about how you will remind him or her of the skill when your child forgets, repeats, or is about to repeat, his or her undesired behaviour.

If no such agreement is made with the child in advance, there is a high risk that when the child forgets his or her skill, you will become frustrated and respond by criticising or scolding the child:

- Oh, my. Now you are biting your nails again.
- Didn't we just agree that you will stop bothering your baby brother?
- What's this? You promised to clean up your mess. Why didn't do it?
- This doesn't seem to work. You are doing it again.
- I should have guessed it. The moment I turn my back, you are doing it again.
- The discussions that we had were apparently just a waste of time. This whole thing is very frustrating to me.

Instead of expressing your frustration to your child, you can decide to tackle setbacks in a way that is consistent with skills thinking. That means that you deliberately refrain from criticising your child and remind him or her of the skill in some special manner that you have developed together with your child.

Make an agreement with your child about how you will remind them if they forget their skill.

The ground rule is that children easily experience straightforward verbal reminders as criticism but respond much better to previously agreed-upon gestures, signs, or code-words.

A mother told me that her 8-year-old daughter had a bad habit. Whenever the mother asked her daughter to do something – for example, to practise her homework for learning to play violin – the daughter always replied by saying, "In a moment," or "soon," and then dawdled for long periods of time. The daughter's dawdling had become a problem for the mother, as she had ended up repeating her instructions over and over again to get the daughter to take care of her responsibilities. To find a solution to the problem, the mother decided to have a talk with her daughter. She presented the challenge to her daughter like this:

"I am responsible for taking care that you do your violin homework, and I don't mind reminding you about it. But I've noticed that when I remind you, you often respond by saying that you will do it soon. Then you keep on doing something else and I must remind you again and again. I've noticed that you tend to become annoyed when I remind you repeatedly, and I also don't like it when I have to remind you about the same thing many times. I think we should find a better way to handle those situations."

When the mother noticed that her daughter was listening, she suggested, "How would you want me to remind you to practice the violin? What if I don't say anything but I show you some sign that will tell you it's time to get your violin and start practising?"

The mother's suggestion led to a conversation that ended in an agreement: From then on, the mother would not tell her daughter to start practising but would instead flash her a card with a picture of a violin on it. The daughter agreed that if her mother didn't say anything but showed her the card, it might work better. She even drew the picture of a violin on the card that her mother was supposed to show her. The card signalling method the mother came up with for her daughter didn't solve the problem instantaneously, but the negotiation served as a starting point for a continued conversation that allowed mother and daughter to find better ways to communicate with one another in situations where the mother needed to remind the daughter of her various responsibilities.

Parents and other carers can prevent the vicious cycle of reminding and dawdling by inviting children to participate in finding a way to remind the child of a skill that is agreeable to him or her. A primary school teacher shared with me the following example of how she has used this idea with her pupils at school.

When 7-year-old first-graders start school in the Fall, they are like angels. The class is quiet, the pupils listen attentively to me and concentrate on their tasks diligently. Gradually, as weeks and months go by, the noise level in the class starts to rise and if I would ignore it, the class would be quite loud and unruly by Christmas. I usually invite the pupils to help me find a solution to the problem. Some time ago, I asked the pupils of my current class if they had noticed that the noise level in the class was higher than it used to be in the Fall when we started. The students agreed with me that this was the case. I then asked them what they thought I should do to make the class quieter again. I gave them some time to think and after a while, they came up with a suggestion.

"When you notice that one of us is being noisy," they said, "don't say anything to him or her. Just keep on teaching and walk over to the loud pupil and while you are standing beside or behind him or her, lower your hand gently on the pupil's shoulder."

Upon hearing this, my mind's eye conjured up a picture of the poor teacher rushing around the class from student to student laying her hands on their shoulders. "How has that solution worked for you?" I asked.

"It has worked surprisingly well," the teacher told me and pointed out that the suggestion had probably worked well because it came from the pupils and not from herself.

The gentle reminding method works not only with children but also with adults, as the following example illustrates.

The mother of 8-year-old Demian had participated in a weekend workshop on skills thinking in parenting. Upon arrival back home, she wanted to test the approach with her son. The mother showed Demian an illustrated workbook designed for children and managed to get him to volunteer to be his mother's first guinea pig. They quickly found a skill for Demian to learn and were already well on the way towards working on the subsequent steps of the process when Demian suddenly became thoughtful and began staring at his mother. "What now, what are you thinking about?" the mother asked him.

"Mom, I think you should also learn a skill," he said.

"You think so? What skill do I need to learn?" asked his mother.

"You often yell at me. You should learn to speak to me nicely even if you are angry at me," explained Demian.

The mother felt a twinge of guilt in her heart. "True," she said, "I do sometimes get angry and yell at you. I don't want to do it. I will try to learn to speak nicely to you."

The fact that mother and son were both learning a skill made it possible for them to be supporters of each other. When it was time to talk about how they wanted to be reminded of their skills when needed, Demian looked at his mother and said, "If you forget your skill and start yelling at me again, I can remind you with a hand gesture."

"That's a good idea," said his mother. "Which hand gesture will you use?" the mother wanted to know.

"I will show you this sign," Demian said, and brought his hands together to form his fingers into the shape of a heart. The mother was moved by her son's touching proposal and readily agreed to it.

The rationale behind the gentle reminding method is founded in the following idea: When the person in question – whether a child or an adult – has offered a suggestion for a way for others to remind him or her of a particular skill, it is then difficult for him or her to become annoyed for being reminded about the skill. The person in question is likely at least trying to respond positively to a reminder proposed by him or herself.

Let me conclude this step 4 by repeating the words that you may find useful in initiating a conversation with your child about gentle reminders.

You have already become quite good at _____, but sometimes you still forget. If I notice that you forget, I can remind you in some way. How do you want me to do it?

One of the additional benefits of gentle reminders is that if the way in which you have agreed with your child to remind him or her doesn't give the desired effect, it is easy for you to continue the conversation with your child. You may say, for example, "I have tried to remind you a few times in the way that you said you'd like me to do it, but it hasn't always worked. Let's try to find a better way for me to remind you. What do you suggest?"

Step 5. Reinforce your child's learning

"I'll give you 10 Euros for each A that you bring home from school," is a sentence that many a parent has uttered to their child. It is not uncommon for parents to try to motivate their children to learn or to improve their performance by promising to give them money, sweets, or other rewards if they succeed. Offering to reward children in this way sounds rational, but the method doesn't work as well as one might assume. I remember reading about a psychological field study where the researchers offered to give a group of teenagers a considerable amount of money if they could succeed in raising their marks at school to a certain degree at the end of the semester. All the students in the research group were eager to accept the challenge and felt confident that they would be able to accomplish the task. Despite the fact that the reward offered to the students was a considerable sum of money, none of them succeeded in attaining the goal at the end of the semester. The researchers concluded that motivating children with money does not bring about desired results.

Reinforce motivation by awakening your child's interest in learning the skill.

Many currently popular parenting approaches rely on the idea that children's motivation to change their behaviour is best enhanced by a clever and consistent use of rewards and consequences. Skills thinking is based on very different theory motivation that doesn't operate with rewards and consequences, but on collaboration; on finding ways to raise the child's interest in learning skills and nurturing the child's motivation to learn the skill by using a wide range of tools, ranging from letting the child name their skill to engaging supporters, and from taking help from power creatures to celebrating the child's successes and progress. Let's take a closer look at the diverse motivational strategies that are distinctive of the skills approach.

Praise the child verbally

Small children enjoy straightforward verbal praise, which means saying to the child something along the lines of, "Well done," "You did it," "You have learned so much," "I am proud of you," or "I am impressed." Such responses are a sign to the child that you appreciate their efforts, and you are impressed by their progress. However, when children grow older, they tend to start to perceive straightforward praise as patronising. If you can spot signs of this happening, you should shift to using one of the many other options discussed below.

Praise the child discreetly

Instead of using straightforward praise, you can show your appreciation to your child with a designated hand gesture, facial expression or mutually agreed upon code word. You may, for example, show your child the thumbs up sign, or give a high-five or a tap on the shoulder. An experienced youth leader once said that most teenagers today are allergic to verbal praise, but they respond well to tacit signs of appreciation.

Praise the child for trying

- Good try!
- Give it one more go!

- You tried your best!
- Next time you will do it!
- It's getting better and better!
- It was close!
- You are tenacious!
- You don't give up easily!

Even if the child does not succeed in practising their skill, you should still consider praising the child for trying: "It didn't quite work out yet, but we could all see that you tried your best. Don't worry, you will soon get the hang of it."

When your child realizes that you don't only appreciate their successes, but also their attempts and efforts, it will motivate them to try even harder next time.

Share the child's progress with other people

Instead of praising the child directly, you can accomplish much by praising the child to someone else. Supposing you are the mother, you would be speaking on the phone with your mother. You could say to her something like, "Did I already tell you that Sue has learned to eat vegetables? Yesterday she ate the first carrot of her life, not just a little piece but the entire carrot." If your daughter eavesdrops on you and hears what you said, she will be happy, perhaps even happier than if you had said the same thing to her directly. In addition, your mother is likely to report the good news back to your daughter at some point later: "I head from your mother that you have eaten an entire carrot. She was very happy when she told me, and I also think it's a great achievement!"

Consult the child

"I try to praise my son when he acts the way I want him to, but he doesn't like me praising him at all. Instead of becoming happy, he becomes irritated and tells me to stop saying anything of the kind to him."

I have often heard parents wonder why their child, who is usually a teenager, but can also be a smaller child, consistently rejects their parents' praise. If your child doesn't appear to like you praising them, you may want to ask them how they want you to praise them. "I've noticed that you don't always like my way of praising you, but when I notice that you are doing something right and I feel proud of you, I would like to show it to you in some way. How do you want me to do it? How do you want me to tell you that I'm proud of you?" Your children need you to praise them when they learn skills, and if your way of praising them doesn't work with them, ask them to advise you how to do it in a way that suits them better.

Ask questions about the child's progress

Asking your child questions about their successes and progress is an elegant and effective way of ensuring that they feel that you appreciate their learning. In this approach, you don't praise the child directly, but you ask them questions to invite them to account for their achievements: "Seems like you managed to do your homework today right after returning home from school. That's not easy. How did you do it?"

Questions that invite the child to think about how they managed to act in the desirable manner convey the message that you appreciate them for their accomplishment.

Plan to celebrate

Many years ago, when we worked on developing the skills-oriented approach with a small group of special needs children, we came across a fun way to help children feel proud of their progress. We started to arrange weekly celebrations where we celebrated with soft drinks and cake when one of the children in the group had learned his or her skill. On one Friday, we would celebrate a child who used to be desperately slow at putting on his clothes, but had now learned to dress himself quickly, and the next Friday we would arrange a celebration for another child who had learned the skill of eating around the same table with others. It was a surprise to us how important the celebration ritual was for the children. They eagerly waited for their celebration and there was no doubt that the anticipation of the celebration was a major motivator for the children to learn their skills.

A mother told me that she had tried for weeks in vain to get her 4-year-old daughter to sleep in her own bed. She had explained to her daughter why it was important for her to learn to sleep in her own bed, and she had promised to reward her with gifts, but her motivational tactics had not done the trick. She had seen a TV program about the skills approach and even if the method seemed quite complicated to her, she did remember one of the steps discussed in the program - the step of making a plan together with the child about how to celebrate when the child has learned the skill. When she talked about the issue next time with her daughter, she said, "If you succeed in sleeping in your own bed 7 nights in a row, we can arrange a party to honour your accomplishment."

To the mother's surprise, her daughter responded with excitement to the idea, saying, "Can we invite grandma?" She took great pleasure in planning the upcoming celebration with her mother. When the mother told me about her experience, her daughter had already succeeded in sleeping through the night in her own bed 4 days in a row.

The celebration also offers an opportunity for the child to show their appreciation to all their supporters who have in various ways helped and supported them in learning the skill. Thanking supporters cultivates feelings of gratitude, intensifies bonds between people and adds to the child's motivation to maintain the skill that they have learned.

It may seem at first that celebration is just another way of rewarding the child for their accomplishment, and in a sense that's true, but I prefer to think of it as a ritual, or rite of passage, that reinforces the child's learning and changes the way the child is viewed by other people. The celebration is a symbolic indication of growth, maturation and development.

Next skill for the child to learn

A child's life is a process of continuous learning. When your child has learned one skill, it's time to start learning another. Moving on from learning one skill to learning the next one is a source of pride for the child, a sign that one challenge has been conquered and the child is all set to encounter the next one.

Use certificates

Most children like the idea of getting a certificate, badge, medal or some other related indication they have acquired a skill. The expectation of earning such a recognition for achievement adds to the child's motivation to make the effort needed to learn the skill. Most children like to hear an adult tell them something along the lines of: "When you have learned your skill, you get a badge like this that you can wear on your chest," or "When you have learned that skill, you can get this certificate that you can hang on your wall."

Badges and certificates are representations of social respect and appreciation.

* * *

By now you are quite familiar with the principles of the skills approach; you know how to convert your child's challenges into skills he or she can learn, you are familiar with a number of ways to motivate your child to learn those skills, and you may even have attached a sheet of paper on your refrigerator door to remind yourself of the guidelines that help you put the ideas into practice in your day-to-day life with your child. It is now time to invite you to move on to the next chapter in which I will present to you a collection of illustrative case examples, inspiring true stories describing how parents, teachers and other people involved in raising children have succeeded in helping children overcome diverse challenges using the skills approach.

6

EXAMPLES

The skills approach in action

Praise for trying – not just for succeeding.

DOI: 10.4324/9781003435723-6

The best way to learn to use any new method or approach is to first observe someone else using the method and then use the method yourself. If that is not possible, the second-best way, I suppose, to learn a method is to hear stories of how someone used the method and then try the method yourself.

This chapter consists of a collection of true stories about how skills orientation was used to help children of diverse ages conquer different types of challenges ranging from minor difficulties to more serious mental health issues.

Over the years I have come across numerous such stories. Most of them are written by people who have participated in a training workshop on using skills orientation with children. Submitting such a report is the final step in the certification process.

Selective eating, 4-year-old girl

Linda's mother took part in a workshop to learn about the skills approach. When coming home, she told Linda about what she had learned and asked her if she'd like to try the method with her. Linda agreed but was unable to say right away what skill she wanted to learn. Later that day, as she was having her evening meal, she told her mom that she wanted to learn to taste new foods. Linda was very selective with foods and was very suspicious about trying new foods.

Linda named her skill yum-yum-skill. She thought this was an important skill for her to learn because she remembered that she had often felt sad when she had not dared to taste some new food that others had found delicious. She could also recall a few times when she had been brave enough to taste something new and then found it to be good.

As her supporters, Linda wanted to have her parents and her two brothers. As her fantasy helper, she wanted to have Sniff from the stories of the Moomin Valley. Sniff is fond of treats and always hungry. Her mother got Linda a plate, a mug and a spoon decorated with an image of Sniff.

Linda was keen to talk about her skill to everyone who happened to visit the family and she wanted to demonstrate her skill by tasting whatever new flavours were served at the table. She also wanted her parents to buy products from the supermarket that she had not previously tasted, such as new varieties of yogurt and fruits that were new to her.

In order for Linda's parents to help her not to forget her skill, it was agreed that they would use the code-word "yum-yum." Linda was very motivated to learn her skill and she courageously tasted new flavours.

There were no real setbacks, but the code word "yum-yum" worked well to encourage her when there were opportunities for her to taste something that she would be reluctant to try. Sweet flavours were easier. With savoury flavours, Linda needed more encouragement. Linda acquired dozens of new flavours during her training period. Pear yogurt, mandarins, and spinach soup became her new favourites. Olives, blue cheese, and cabbage soup remained no-go, but even these Linda tried to taste a few times.

Learning the skill went smoothly, and in a month the family celebrated Linda's success with a delicacy party. At the party, Linda served her supporters various delicacies, some of which were new. As a token of thanks, she drew each of her supporters a picture of their favourite delicacy.

Linda's brothers, who had been supporting her, had also learned to taste new foods because Linda had encouraged them to try the new and unfamiliar flavours. When Linda tasted olives, she managed to encourage her mother to taste them too. When they tasted olives together, they had some good laughs at each other's grimaces.

Having learned the "yum-yum" skill, Linda wants to start learning another skill. She has already decided that when she has learned her next skill, she wants to have a princess party.

Selective eating and pooping in pants, 5-year-old boy

Allan attended speech therapy due to his delayed speech development, but he also had other challenges. One of them was that he was very picky with eating. Due to his inadequate diet, he was often hungry and cranky. His picky eating had caused him constipation. He also had frequent stomach aches and constipation, which in turn had made him avoid going to the toilet, with the result that he frequently pooed into his trousers. In kindergarten, Allan refused to eat with other children at the table. During lunchtime he hid behind the door and refused to come out before the table was cleaned up.

Allan's speech therapist had a meeting with the staff of the kindergarten. In the meeting it was decided that the first skill for Allan to learn was to eat lunch at the table together with other children. This was such a big skill for Allan that the teachers decided to divide it into smaller steps, the first being to learn to participate in setting the table with the other children.

Allan quickly learned to participate in setting the table and was praised by the staff and his parents for his accomplishment. His next small skill was to learn to sit together with the other children at the table during lunch without having to eat anything. When he mastered that skill, he moved on to taking some food on his plate without having to eat it. In this way, Allan progressed step-by-step until, before long, he managed to eat together with the other children.

Once the eating problem had been conquered with the skills approach, Allan's parents brought up the toilet problem with the speech therapist. Together they talked with Allan and proposed to him that he would learn to go regularly to the toilet. Allan agreed. He understood that not only would it make his parents happy, but it would also help him avoid his tummy aches and be in a better mood in the kindergarten.

When asked who he wanted to support him, Allan named his parents, grandmother, and speech therapist. As his power creature, he wanted to have his favourite Lego toy character. Allan's mother promised him that she would buy him that Lego character toy when he learns to go regularly on the toilet.

Allan practised his skill by sitting some time on the toilet every day. His mother encouraged him by staying close to him and praising him, regardless of whether or not he succeeded in producing anything in the toilet.

Allan learned the skill of defecating into the toilet in a couple of weeks. His mother bought him the Poop-King toy, as promised, and Allan presented it proudly to his other supporters. He was so proud of his accomplishment that he wanted to teach his skill to others as well. "Look, you can also get a cool Lego character like this if you learn to go to toilet," he was overheard explaining to his 2-year-old cousin when she was visiting them with her parents.

Day wetting, 6-year-old boy

Sunny wet his trousers almost daily. He was so lively that he simply didn't have enough patience to go to the toilet to pee. His twin brother Walter poked fun at him and his problem by calling him "Wee-Sunny."

Sunny's parents suggested to him that he learn the skill of taking breaks during play in order to go to the toilet to wee. Because Sunny and Walter were together practically all the time, a plan was drawn up together with them whereby the boys would take breaks together. Sunny would learn to go to wee, and Walter would not have to suffer from the nuisance of the smell of wee in his nose.

Both boys wanted to give the skill a name. Sunny called his skill "ants in the pants," and Walter called it "Little tree" after a popular air freshener brand for cars. Sunny's supporters were mom, dad, Walter, big brother (whom the twins looked up to), grandparents, and Aunt Hanna with her two daughters, who were a couple of years older than the twins. As his power creature, Sunny wanted Spiderman because he was a Spiderman fan and liked to wear a Spiderman outfit.

Sunny wanted to organise a costume party when he had learned his skill. Both boys became excited about the thought and planned to dress as Spiderman at the event.

Sunny practised diligently with the support of his twin brother and his big brother. He often brought up the subject at breakfast, suggesting that the boys draw up a plan together about how many breaks they would take during the day and when those beaks would take place. Aunt Hanna made Sunny an "Ants-in-the-Pants" poster, where Sunny was allowed to paste a star sticker in the evening if he had practised his skill of taking breaks that day. He got a sticker for practising his skill regardless of whether or not he had wet his pants that day. The sticker was earned for keeping breaks – not for keeping dry.

It only took two weeks for Sunny to learn to take breaks, to wee in the toilet instead of his trousers, and to stay dry all day long for several days in a row. The celebration was organized, and all of Sunny's supporters turned up in a costume – including grandpa who surprised everyone by wearing a bunny costume. Aunt Hanna baked a Spiderman cake and big brother took Sunny on a ride on his new motorcycle.

Refusal to use hearing aid, 7-year-old boy

Joe had a mild hearing disability. He had recently gotten hearing aids to be used at school. The problem was that Joe kept removing the hearing aids from his ears during the school day. This was not good because to get used to wearing hearing aids, one needs to use them all day long. Also, when Joe didn't wear his hearing aids, he couldn't hear his teacher which led to him becoming restless and disruptive in the class.

When asked why he kept removing his hearing aids, he said, "I don't know. I can't help it. It happens automatically." Joe's audiologist decided to use the skills approach to help Joe learn the skill of wearing his hearing aids throughout the day.

In a meeting with Joe and his parents, the audiologist first asked about Joe's skills, abilities, and hobbies. Joe was a skilful soccer player and an expert on soccer. He could, for example, name all the players on the FC Barcelona team by heart. When the audiologist asked him what skill he needed to become better at, he said he wanted to learn to keep his hearing aids on all day. He knew that this was an important skill for him to learn. Keeping his hearing aids on all day would allow him to hear what his teachers were saying, his marks would probably improve, and he wouldn't have to always sit in the front row in class.

"Let's give a name for your skill," said the audiologist. "What do you want to call it?"

It was not a surprise that Joe wanted to call his skill "Messi" after his football superstar. For his supporters, he wanted to have his parents, his PE teacher, and one of his classmates. His power creature was Superman. He explained that Superman has super hearing and can hear people's cries for help from far away.

The audiologist offered to give Joe a special certificate of achievement when he learned his Messi skill, but Joe was not interested in certificates. Instead, he wanted to get a trophy, something similar that the winning team gets in world soccer tournaments. Joe's parents agreed to make him one from paper mâché.

"How do you want your classmate and your teacher to remind you if they see you removing your hearing aids from your ears?" asked the audiologist.

Joe explained that he wanted them to do it discreetly by whispering the word "Messi" to him.

After the meeting, Joe's parents bought Joe a baseball cap embellished with an image of Superman. Joe loved his Superman cap and wore it at school every day. His parents also gave him a notebook to keep a log of his progress and to allow them to praise him each time he managed to break his previous record of keeping his hearing aids on.

At school, when his classmates saw his Superman cap, they asked him about it. He explained that his parents had given it to him to remind him to wear his hearing aids at school. This encouraged his classmates to ask him questions about his hearing handicap. He was not able to answer all their questions, so his parents suggested that he ask the teacher for permission to give the class a talk about his disability. Joe asked his audiologist to join him and together the two of them spoke to the class. The classmates listened to them attentively and everyone was willing to support him in remembering to keep his hearing aids on in class. The audiologist brought along a special headset that all the students in the class could try on to get a sense of how it feels to listen to sound through a hearing aid.

A few weeks later it had become evident that Joe had learned the Messi skill and it was time to celebrate his achievement.

Fear of dogs, 7-year-old boy

Sam was afraid of dogs to the extent that he had to turn down his classmates' invitations to their birthday parties if the family owned a dog. Sam's mother, who had learned about the skills approach, suggested to him that he might want to try to overcome his fear of dogs with the help of this method. Sam became interested in the idea. He understood that overcoming his fear meant that he could take part in his friends' birthday parties and that he would be able to play with his cousins when he visited his auntie's house, where they had two small dogs.

"What skill do you need to learn in order to overcome your fear of dogs?" his mother asked Sam.

"I need to learn to let dogs come close to me and let them sniff me," Sam answered. His mother was impressed by his answer. It seemed to confirm the assertion that converting challenges into skills comes naturally to children.

As his supporters, Sam wanted to have his mother, father, grandmother, and the two sisters with whom he often played, who lived just across the street from their house. He named his skill "Tucker skill." When his mother asked him how he wished to celebrate learning his skill, he said he wanted to invite all his supporters to a party where everyone would have a chance to enjoy his favourite delicacy, grandma's carrot cake.

The next day, Sam saw through the window that one of their neighbours was walking their dog on the street just outside their house. "C'mon, let's go!" he said to his mother.

"Where do you want us to go?" asked his mother.

"Our neighbour is walking their dog on the street. I want to go to practise my skill."

They went together to the street to greet the dog and its owner. Sam assumed a squatting position, covered his face with his hands, and allowed the dog to sniff him for a while.

"You did it. Well done, Sam!" said his mother in awe when Sam got up and the dog walked on with its owner.

"Yes, I know," said Sam with a proud look on his face. He continued in the same breath, "Let's call Grandma and tell her what I just did!"

When Sam had practised his skill on several occasions for a few weeks, he had learned his skill and overcome his fear of dogs. One day, a week or two after the party had been arranged, his mother noticed out of the corner of her eye that Sam was teaching his newly learned skill to his 3-year-old younger brother with the help of a cuddly toy.

"Pretend that this is a dog," he explained to his brother, "and allow it to sniff you like this. You have nothing to be afraid of. In this way you can get used to it and you don't need to fear it at all."

Sam's mother found Sam's eagerness to pass his newly acquired skill to his brother amusing because his brother had never been afraid of dogs.

Biting nails, 7-year-old boy

A mother was inspired by the skills approach and wanted to try it with her son, Dan. She told him about the idea of overcoming challenges by learning skills and asked him if he had a problem that he would want to solve using the approach.

"I don't have any problems," Dan said to his mother.

"You don't need to have any problems," his mother explained. "We just need to find some skill for you to learn."

"Okay," said Dan, "in that case I would want to learn to stop biting my nails."

"That's a good idea, Dan," his mother said, "but what skill do you think you need to learn to stop biting your nails?"

After giving the question some thought, they concluded that the skill Dan needed to learn was to "take good care of my nails."

"Do you want to have a power animal that will help you take good care of your nails?" asked his mother. Dan's eyes lit up. He thought about a few different animals and ended up with a chameleon. It was a cartoon character from one of his favourite picture books. Dan drew a picture of the chameleon and while drawing he also came up with a name for his skill. The name was "Flick," the name of the chameleon in the book.

When his mother asked Dan how he would want to celebrate learning the skill, he didn't need to think for long. He wanted to organise a party at home, invite all his supporters, and also his aunt and uncle. He wanted cake to be served and a board game to be played.

As his supporters, Dan wanted to have his mother, father, grandfather, grandmother, and both of his brothers. Together with his mother he wrote a letter to all his supporters. It said: "Dear supporter, you can help me to learn to take good care of my nails. If you sometimes see that I forget my skill, you can say to me "Flick." When I have learned to take good care of my nails, I will invite you to a party that I hope you will come to."

"I wonder if we can figure out a way for you to practise your skill," said his mother. "What can you do to learn to take good care of your nails?"

Dan explained that for him the most challenging situations were those in which he needed to do something within a fixed time; for example, when he was supposed to complete a set of algebra problems in 5 minutes. Based on this observation, Dan and his mother designed an exercise. His mother gave Dan a problem that he was supposed to complete within a set timeframe without biting his nails. His mother used her phone to capture Dan's performance on video. It was obvious from watching the video that Dan was struggling hard to maintain his skill while performing the task. Even though he brought his fingers to his mouth a couple of times, he succeeded in refraining from biting his nails.

Dan decided to practise his skill by repeating daily the exercise that had been recorded on video. He planned to post a picture of the chameleon next to his desk at home so that he could remind himself of his skill by glancing occasionally at the picture. For school Dan drew a small picture of the chameleon that he kept in his pencil case and placed on his desk during lessons to remind him of his skill.

In addition to this, his mother helped Dan create a poster for his skill. In the centre of the poster was a picture of a treasure chest. The idea was that when his mother would cut Dan's nails, they would be collected and glued onto the treasure chest on the poster.

When Dan and his mother told the rest of the family about the plan and showed them the letter they had written, everyone said they wanted to support Dan. In fact, they were all so impressed by the plan that they too started to talk about skills that they might need to learn and about possible power creatures that might help them learn those skills.

When Dan sat down next time to follow up on his nail-project a week later, he proudly presented his hands to his mother: He had succeeded in growing four nails! Dan allowed his mother to cut the

4 nails with nail scissors. The 4 cut nails were glued, as planned, into the treasure chest on Dan's poster.

"You succeeded in growing 4 nails," said his mother, "and I feel confident that you will succeed in growing more. What about you? Do you feel confident that you can do it?"

"I can do it because I'm smart and I have good imagination," Dan said.

The planned celebration took place when his mother had cut Dan's nails 3 times. When asked what skill he wanted to learn next, Dan mentioned his habit of spinning hair around his finger while he was concentrating on doing something that required his full attention. Because of this habit he had an almost bald spot on one side of his head. He was determined to conquer this bad habit using the same approach he had used to conquer his habit of biting his nails.

Low self-esteem, 8-year-old girl

Amanda suffered from low self-esteem. She couldn't see anything good about herself and she was convinced that she would never succeed at anything. During recess she was rude to other pupils, calling them names and getting constantly into fights with them. Her parents and her teachers had made many attempts to talk with her about her attitude, but so far nothing had helped. She had also gotten warnings, and she had been punished for her rude behaviour towards her classmates, but consequences had not had any effect on her.

The classroom teacher in Amanda's class was interested in the skills approach and wanted to try the idea with Amanda. She asked Amanda to have a one-on-one talk with her during the school day after one of the lessons.

"Amanda, I would like you to learn a skill that I think would be important for you to learn," she said. Amanda was listening. "I want you to start paying attention to things that you do that you succeed at. I am going to give you this diary and I want you to write something in it every day. I want you to write every day one thing – however small – that you have done that went well, that you succeeded in doing." The teacher was unsure whether Amanda understood what she was exactly supposed to learn, but she nevertheless succeeded in getting Amanda to give a name to the skill of paying attention to her small successes. The skill was to be called "Princess-skill." Amanda admired various teenage celebrities, princesses, and just about anything that was pretty and girly.

Practising the Princess-skill turned out to be challenging for Amanda. The next day the teacher met with Amanda at the end of the school day to see what she had managed to write into her diary. Amanda had not succeeded in reporting any successes. The teacher realized that she had given Amanda an assignment that was too difficult for her to carry out. She realized that Amanda needed some assistance to be able to do the assignment. The teacher sat down with Amanda to review her day and to identify a few things that had happened that could be seen as small successes. The same happened the next day. Amanda had not managed to identify any successes and the page that was reserved for that day in her diary was empty. Again, the teacher helped her review her day and to find something to write into the diary. It took one whole week before Amanda started to get the hang of it and finally managed to write something in her diary on her own without her teacher helping her.

Amanda worked on her Princess diary for three more weeks with the support of her teacher. The teacher gave her an embossed sticker each time she managed to write a few lines of text into her diary describing something she had succeeded with. Amanda decorated her diary with the embossed scraps she got from her teacher and a few weeks later they both agreed that Amanda had learned the Princess skill.

Amanda's progress was slow, but not long after starting with the project the teacher heard from some of Amanda's classmates that they had observed some changes in her. According to her classmates, she started to smile during recess and the badmouthing she was notorious for had diminished considerably.

When Amanda's teacher asked her later if there was another skill that she wanted to learn, she said she wanted to learn to give compliments to her classmates and to tell nice things about them to her teacher. She had already decided to call this skill "the Queen skill."

When Amanda changed schools the following year, her teacher from the new school called the teacher at her previous school to find out what Amanda meant by asking her when she could start learning a new skill. According to the teacher she had even given a name to her next skill. It was to be called "the Cindy skill."

Cursing, 8-year-old boy

Adam had been referred to a family guidance clinic evaluation because of problems related to attention and impulsivity. There he had been given the diagnosis of ADHD. At school Adam was criticized, among other things, for constant cursing. His mother was worried about his bad language but talking to him about it, or reprimanding him, had had no effect on his behaviour. Adam was himself not proud of his swearing, but he felt that the habit was beyond his control.

Adam's mother decided to talk about his cursing to the occupational therapist who Adam met with regularly. She was interested in the skills approach and offered to try to help Adam to give up his offensive language.

"What words could you use instead of swearwords when you become angry?" she asked Adam.

"I could say "teddy" instead," Adam suggested.

"That's a great idea," the therapist said. "You could pick up the habit of saying "teddy bear" whenever there is something that annoys you."

Adam was crazy about teddy bears and therefore it was no wonder that he wanted to call the skill "teddy bear skill." When the therapist asked him what good it would do to him to stop swearing and to become good at the teddy bear skill, he said, "My teacher and my mother wouldn't get mad at me so often."

As his power creature he wanted to have one of his favourite teddy bears. "How can your teddy bear help you remember to say "teddy" instead of using swear words?" asked the therapist. This question sparked a conversation that led to a couple of useful ideas. The teddy bear was placed on Adam's bed to remind him of his teddy bear skill, and at school a picture of a teddy bear that had been cut out of paper was attached with tape onto the lid of his desk.

In addition to his therapist, Adam's supporters included his mother, his teacher, and his father who lived in another city. Also, his grandmother was informed, but her ability to support him was limited because she lived far away. The therapist suggested that Adam invite a few of his classmates to support him, but Adam was not willing to do it. The therapist thought that his reluctance to engage with his friends was a sign that he felt embarrassed of his bad habit.

At first Adam was keen on developing his teddy bear skill, and each time he managed to avoid using swearwords by saying "teddy" instead, his supporters rewarded him with praise. He loved parties and became quite excited when he learned that it would be possible to celebrate his success in some way when he had learned his skill. Not surprisingly, he wanted to plan the celebration to the theme of teddy bears. Guests would naturally be served teddy gummies and they would play a party game called "teddy's tail," in which blind-folded players tried to attach the teddy bear's tail to the right spot on a picture of a teddy bear.

That Adam would stop swearing entirely seemed unrealistic, but even just reducing swearing considerably was considered an achievement worthy of celebration. Adam practised his teddy bear skill with the help of a role-play with his occupational therapist at the clinic and with his mother at home. The role-play involved staging all kinds of situations in which Adam pretended to be irritated and then, instead of cursing, he embellished his language with the word "teddy" or "teddy bear." Adam liked the game, and it was therefore not difficult to get him to agree to play it.

Adam experienced frequent setbacks, but the skills approach helped his supporters to relate to him differently. When Adam forgot his skill at home and began to swear again with a loud voice, his mother reminded him of his teddy bear skill by holding Adam's power teddy in her hands and showing it to him. At school the picture of a teddy served a similar function, as it gave his teacher the option of not saying anything but simply pointing to the picture of the teddy instead.

Gradually Adam's swearing lessened to the extent that the planned party could be arranged. He had also succeeded in gathering an impressive collection of teddy bear stickers that his mother had given to him every time he succeeded in replacing swearwords with "teddy bear."

The party was held, and it was a success. After everyone had had some cake, Adam thanked both his mother and his occupational therapist for their support. When the therapist asked him what skill he would want to learn next, Adam explained to her that his mother had the bad habit of calling other drivers in traffic idiots and suggested that his mother learn the skill of replacing the word "idiot" with the word "sausage." Adam's mother agreed to his proposal, and he promised to remind her to help her remember to replace "idiot" with "sausage" while driving in traffic.

His mother, on her part, told the therapist that Adam had a bad habit of waking up at night and crawling into her bed, which was a problem because she usually woke up and often found it difficult to go to sleep again. Adam understood that his mother deserved to have a good night's sleep, but was nevertheless not keen on learning to sleep in his own bed through the night. However, he agreed to the plan that a mattress would be placed on his mother's bedroom floor, and he would learn to crash on the mattress instead of crawling into his mother's bed.

Concentration problem, 9-year-old boy

Tom had been placed in a small special class due to his impulsivity. He had the bad habit of shouting out with a loud voice whatever thoughts happened to come to his mind. And when he began talking, it was difficult to interrupt him or to make him stop. His manner of communication was disturbing other pupils and led to numerous arguments and fights with his fellow classmates.

Another challenge of Tom's was that it was very difficult for him to concentrate on listening to his teacher. His own thoughts appeared to race so fast that he often failed to hear what the teacher had just said. If the teacher, or the teacher's assistant, tried to find out from him whether he had heard the teacher's instruction, he tended to become irritated and began to blame the adult for bugging him.

Tom's third challenge was that he did not tolerate his teacher, or the assistant teacher, helping him with his assignments. When they tried, he began to crank and speak rudely to the teacher or the assistant teacher. Even an adult standing near him observing him working on his task was enough to irritate him when he himself felt that he didn't need any help.

All the pupils in the special class were learning skills guided by the teacher. Tom's first skill was called "note skill." The purpose of the skill was to help him overcome his habit of calling out his thoughts in a high voice during lessons. This is what he wrote about the note skill into his notebook.

> "When during the lesson something important pops into my mind that I would want to say immediately to the teacher, instead of saying it, I write it on a notepad that I have on my desk. After the lesson I can go to the teacher to tell her what I had in mind. Even if I cannot say immediately what I have in mind, I don't become nervous because the note helps me remember what I wanted to say. I have been amazed at the number of notes that I have written. My classmates say that my skill has had a calming effect on the whole class because many times the things that I say have to do with microcircuits and electronics rather than with what is being taught during the lesson. I have also concentrated better during the lessons now, as I have been able to put aside the things that pop up in my mind. I have noticed that I do not always need to go to the teacher after the lesson to tell her about the things I have written in my notes. It has been sufficient for me to write my thoughts down for myself. I have also enjoyed reading my notes afterwards."

Tom's second skill was related to his difficulty concentrating on following his teachers' instructions. He called this "the robot skill." It meant that after the teacher had given the pupils in the class an instruction, she turned to Tom and asked him if he had heard and understood the instruction. If he had, he answered the teacher in a robot-like voice: "Instruction copied!" As one might guess, Tom was very interested in robots, and for him talking in a robot-like voice was so much fun that he looked forward to the teacher giving instructions to the class.

Tom's third skill was called "Help-skill." It had to do with his difficulty with accepting help from adults. Together with his teacher he found a way of practising his Help-skill. He laminated a card, which he had coloured orange on one side and green on the other. On the orange side he had written in large text, "Please help!" and on the green side, "No thanks, no help needed right now."

The colourful card helped the teacher and the assistant teacher see from a distance when Tom needed help and when he didn't want anyone to help him. In this way, nobody needed to go next to him to see how he was managing his assignments. With the help of the card Tom learned to ask for help, and to refuse help, appropriately and in an acceptable fashion.

Tom learned many skills during the school year. By the end of the following year, he had made so much progress that he was transferred from the special education class to a regular class.

Meltdowns, 9-year-old boy

Marco suffered from meltdowns, or temper tantrums. This meant he had the habit of reacting to disappointments in an emotional way that was way out of proportion with whatever had happened that had provoked the reaction. Even minor frustrations and ordinary everyday challenges in the classroom were overwhelming to Marco and enough to cause him to have a meltdown.

Marco's teacher had a one-on-one talk with him. She asked him what skill he needed to learn to be happier at school. Marco explained that he "wanted to stop feeling frustrated and crying." He said crying made him feel "down and unable to do anything about the situation."

"So, tell me, Marco, what do you need to learn that will help you to stop feeling frustrated and crying? What do you need to learn to do instead in situations that are difficult for you to handle?" the teacher asked. This was by no means a simple question for Marco, but after a while, with a little help from his teacher, he concluded that he needed to learn to "ask for help" in situations that were difficult for him. And to ask for help he needed to learn to raise his hand to signal to the teacher that he needed help.

"I think that's a really good idea, Marco. You will surely benefit from learning to do that. And what will you call that skill? What shall we call the skill that you need to learn?"

"The helping hand skill," Marco said.

"That makes sense," said the teacher. "The helping hand skill will help you convert your meltdown moments into moments of guidance and support. I think it's a lovely idea. Perhaps you should also pick a superhero that will help you learn the skill and remind you of your skill when you feel like crying and shouting."

Marco found the idea appealing. He chose a cool and composed superhero from one of his favourite computer games and used the computer skilfully to create an image where his superhero was standing proudly with his hand raised. He pasted the image onto his desk to support him and to remind him of his skill.

His superhero was certainly useful for him, but even more useful was the support and help that he got from his peers. All the other pupils in the class were excited to play their part in helping him. They knew that it was difficult for Marco to control his emotions and understood that he might indeed benefit from developing the helping hand skill, or the skill of requesting help when he felt overwhelmed.

It took time to get Marco to remember to use the helping hand skill, but even if slow, his progress was steady. He himself came up with the idea of sitting next to the teacher in the classroom so that it would be easier for him to request help from her when needed. Gradually Marco began to realise that he could do things without having to burst out shouting and crying even if he found the task overwhelming. Instead, he could raise his hand and get someone to support and help him. Above all, he no longer needed to feel isolated because of his extra sensitivity. He now had a team of people eager to help and support him.

Marco realised that raising his hand to request support worked well and the teacher could see that he was proud and happy every time he succeeded in doing so. His self-confidence improved to the extent that for the first time he started cutting and pasting his own worksheets and working on his own books in class. To celebrate his achievement Marco chose to watch a movie with his classmates.

The teacher supported Marco's development not only by responding promptly to him when he raised his hand for help, but also by taking photos of his achievements and surprising his parents by emailing the photos to them.

At the time of telling this story the project is still ongoing. The teacher says that she feels proud of Marco's progress. She keeps reminding him daily of the importance of continuing to practice his skill and feels confident that the time will come when Marco can move on to learning some additional skills that he will benefit from having in his life.

Sibling rivalry, 11-year-old girl

One of my best friends asked me to talk to Diana, a lovely girl and the youngest of her 4 daughters. My friend explained to me that she was worried about Diana because she was constantly getting into arguments with her sister who was 2 years older than herself. The arguments were mostly verbal, but there had been incidents when she had hit her sister too. The two older siblings, who had already moved out of the home, were reluctant to come home for Christmas because they detested Diana's aggressive behaviour and couldn't help but react to her behaviour by shouting at her.

I talked with Diana at her home. We began our conversation by talking about regular things such as school and friends. I asked her about Christmas and whether she thought her older siblings would come home for Christmas. She was very much looking forward to seeing them again and getting to hug them. I then asked her about her 2-year older sister. She said that she was her favourite sister, that she loved her very much and enjoyed playing with her.

"What about your sister? Would she agree with you?" I asked her.

"Probably not," she said.

"How come?" I asked.

"Because she thinks I don't love her."

"Why is that?"

"It's because I fight with her all the time."

"You fight with her? How come? You just said she is your favourite sister."

"I fight with her because she picks fights with me. She provokes. She's the one who starts all the fights."

"How does it make you feel when she starts a fight?"

"I don't like it. She makes fun of me. If I don't understand what she says, she is nasty to me."

"And what do you do then?"

"I become angry, and I want to fight with her. I feel like I am not important. I hate being the youngest one in our family!"

"You are right. You are the youngest and it can sometimes be hard to be the youngest, but I don't think we can change that. Is there something else we could change to make you happier?"

"Could you tell her to stop teasing me?"

"I can do that, but do you think it will work? Do you think she will stop provoking you if I tell her to stop teasing you?"

"No, I think she will provoke me even if you tell her to stop. My mother can tell her to stop, but she did already, and it didn't help."

"I have an idea. What if we try to find a skill for you to learn?"

"What kind of skill? How to become better at fighting with her?"

"I don't think that would be a good skill for you to learn. I think it would just make your mother more upset."

"That's true. So, what kind of skill do you mean?"

"What if you learned the skill of reacting without feeling bad? What if you learned to respond to her "insults" in a different way, by just smiling at her or saying something nice to her? If you succeed in doing that, everyone would be happier. What do you think?"

"Okay. It will be fun. I will surprise them all."

"You would certainly surprise everyone. But it's not an easy skill to learn. How could you learn to be more patient with her?"

"I need to learn to think before I say anything."

"That's a smart idea: "to think before saying anything." What should you think about before saying anything?"

"I need to think about how what I say influences my sister. I need to say something that will not provoke or hurt her."

"Would you say that the skill you need to learn is to learn to react thoughtfully? Is that correct?"

"Yes. To learn to react thoughtfully."

Once we had come to an agreement about the skill she would benefit from learning, I asked her about what good learning that skill would do her. She was able to list several things. She said that she would feel better and wouldn't be so angry at her sisters.

Instead of fighting, they would have a laugh at the dinner table, and her older sisters would no longer need to be afraid of visiting home. "If I react with a smile and don't get upset, they will be nicer to me in return," Diana said.

I asked Diana to give a name to her skill, but the idea was not appealing to her.

"I don't want the skill to have any name," she said. "It can just be *how to react thoughtfully.*"

As her supporter she wanted her mother. "I am sure she will be more than happy to support you," I said. "She told me that you are good at learning things. She told me that you learned a difficult kata in your karate class and that you were the first child in your group to learn it."

I then asked Diana how she wanted to celebrate learning the skill. Once again, she turned me down instantly. "I don't want to celebrate," she said. "There is no need to celebrate such a thing."

"Okay, no need to celebrate," I said, "but what about next time we meet, if you have succeeded in developing your skill, we go for a cup of hot chocolate, just the two of us? Deal?"

"Yes, that's a good idea," she said. "I love hot chocolate."

"Will you let your sister know about the skill you are going to learn?" I asked Diana.

"No, I won't. My mother will know about it, but I don't want my sister to know. If she knows, she will just tease me more."

Before we ended our heart-to-heart talk, I invited Diana to role-play with me various provoking scenarios where she had to show me how she could stay calm, react with a smile, or say something funny.

I spoke with Diana about a month later. When I asked her how things were going, she said she was happy because there had not been much fighting between her and her sisters. "I always try to think in advance about how much I love them and to find ways to show them my love." I was delighted to hear the good news and invited her for a nice cup of hot chocolate.

When I met with Diana's mother sometime later, she told me that Diana's behaviour had changed significantly. She had learned to be calm at the dinner table, she made jokes that were not intended as insults, and her general mood at home had improved considerably.

Concentration problem, 12-year-old boy

Walter had been given the diagnosis of ADHD. He was so disruptive in class that his teacher had sent him several times to talk to the principal of the school. His marks were low in comparison to his intelligence. His mother had tried to support him by helping him with his homework in the evenings, sometimes for hours on end. Walter wasn't too bothered about his problems himself. He admitted that his hyperactivity gave him some problems during lessons but pointed out that it also had some benefits. Because of his hyperactive temperament he constantly came up with new ideas and was hugely popular among friends.

Walter sat in a meeting with his parents and his guidance counsellor at school. The conversation revolved around the question of what skills Walter needed to develop in order for his distractibility not to give him so many problems at school. Three such skills were identified: "The ability to stop doing something disturbing," "the skill of returning to class calmly after having been dismissed from class," and "the skill of speaking with nobody else but the teacher during the lessons."

"Which one of these three important skills would you want to focus on?" the teacher asked Walter. He chose to focus on the third skill, the skill of only talking to the teacher during lessons.

The guidance counsellor asked Walter to give a name to the skill, but he declined because he thought that naming the skill was a childish idea. He also showed no interest in choosing a power creature to help him learn his skill. That idea, too, appeared childish to him. Instead, he was keen on discussing the benefits of learning the skill. The teacher wrote down the various benefits that were mentioned in the conversation on a flip chart: The relationship between Walter and his teacher would improve, he would get better grades, he would be more successful in the future at work or college, and above all, he would become more self-confident.

As his supporters Walter wanted to have his parents, his teacher, and two of his classmates. The guidance counsellor helped Walter draft a letter to his teacher to explain to her what skill he was going to learn and request her to keep an eye on his efforts and progress.

Walter also intended to make an agreement with the two classmate supporters that they would help him by deliberately refraining from answering his questions during lessons. The guidance counsellor got permission from Walter to inform two more of his teachers about his project.

The guidance counsellor asked Walter to demonstrate his skill in a role-play in which he was to listen attentively to the guidance counsellor while both of his parents were doing their best to distract him. Walter passed the test with distinction and was praised by his parents and the counsellor.

Walter was genuinely motivated to learn his skill. When he came back home that day, he made a poster for his skill with his parents. It stated the skill that he was learning and had lots of empty space for Walter's parents, and perhaps other people too, to write encouraging words to him.

"Suppose your teacher sometimes sees that you are talking during lessons with some of your classmates. How would you want her to remind you of your skill?" asked the guidance counsellor.

"She moves around the class anyway, so she can come over to me and whisper something to me."

"Okay, and what would you want her to whisper to you?" asked the guidance counsellor.

"She can say to me, "come back."" Walter's proposal was added.

An agreement was made with Walter about how others might remind him of his skill if he sometimes forgot the skill at school. Walter suggested that in that case the teacher could come near to him and whisper to him the words, "come back." This suggestion was added to the letter that was to be given to Walter's teacher.

During the next few weeks, Walter's teacher reported to his parents that he was making progress and getting better grades in exams. His teacher had spoken with the parents and said that Walter had become more attentive and that she had become confident that he would do well in the future.

When there was a consensus that Walter had learned his skill, the guidance counsellor gave him a certificate of achievement. To celebrate his accomplishment, Walter, his parents and his two friends went out for pizza together. In the restaurant Walter thanked both his friends and his parents for supporting him.

Interrupting, 12-year-old girl

Sara had several challenges. She was overweight, she had a short attention span and she often got into fights with her friends. She was diagnosed with ADHD, and she had been recommended medication, but her parents didn't like the idea of putting her on medication.

Sara's teacher invited Sara and her parents to come to the school for a meeting to discuss how the school could best support Sara's learning. The teacher had asked Sara's parents to think in advance about what skills she needed to develop to be more successful at school. The topic had been discussed at home and her mother had written down a few skills that the parents thought Sara might benefit from becoming better at. These included "the skill that I do not interrupt adults when they speak," "the skill to raise my hand in class when I want to speak," "the skill of being kinder towards my brother," (Sara had physically attacked her handicapped brother on repeated occasions) and "the skill of sitting in my place in class for longer periods of time."

"Those are all good skills for Sara to learn," said the teacher. "We just need to decide which one to start with."

The parents gave the question some thought and concluded that for the moment the most important skill for Sara to learn was to not interrupt adults. Sara agreed. She said, "I know I am too impatient."

It was not difficult for Sara to think of what benefits learning the skill would bring: "My friends would respect me more and they would like to be with me more. I think I might even make some new friends. I wouldn't be told off so often at school and I wouldn't be dismissed from class as often. I would be able to listen to the teachers better and I wouldn't be criticized so much anymore."

The teachers suggested Sara give a name to her skill. Sara wanted to call the skill "waiting tone." She explained that often when you call a number there is an automated answering machine that tells you to wait until a person will talk to you. While you are waiting you must listen to some boring music, to a waiting tone.

Sara wanted as her supporters her teacher, both her parents, her maternal and paternal grandmothers, two of her good friends, and her dance instructor. She approached each of them to ask them to support her. All of them said yes.

When the teacher asked Sara if she wanted to have a power creature to help her, she initially didn't understand the idea. The teacher explained to her that a power creature is a cartoon character, or imaginary friend, that reminds her of her skill and gives her extra powers while she is learning her skill. Having heard the teacher's explanation she immediately knew that she wanted a certain horse to be her power creature. The horse she was thinking about was known for its patience and docile character.

"How can the horse help you to learn your skill?" asked the teacher.

"I will keep a picture of the horse in my back pocket and whenever I have to wait for something, I will pull it out from my pocket and keep staring at it until it is my turn," she explained.

"That's a brilliant idea," said the teacher, "but how will you remember to do that?"

"I will say to myself "stop," and pull the picture out of my pocket."

Sara became very excited when the topic of celebration was discussed at the end of the meeting. She wanted to arrange a barbecue party and invite all her supporters and her entire dance team.

"What do you think?" the teacher asked her parents. "Will Sara be able to do it? Will she succeed at learning her waiting tone skill?"

"You will learn it if you want," the parents said to her, "because you are a strong girl and you are our daughter." Sara was beaming as she listened to her parents' encouraging words.

"I think it would be useful if all your classmates knew that you are learning the waiting tone skill. Do you want to tell them yourself or would you prefer me to let them know?" asked the teacher. Sara answered that she wanted her teacher to inform her classmates. She also agreed to the idea that the teacher would place a notebook on her desk where everyone, including Sara herself, could write their observations about Sara's progress.

Sara learned her skill sooner than anyone had expected and the barbecue that was arranged to honour her progress was a great success. When the teacher asked her later what skill she wanted to learn next, she said she wanted to learn to use the waiting tone skill elsewhere also, for example in her dance class, with her friends, and with her brother.

Temper tantrum, 12-year-old girl

The following story was told by a foster father.

We have had foster children in our family for over 20 years. Fanny, who has been diagnosed with both ADHD and Foetal Alcohol Syndrome (FAS), has lived with us for 4 years now. She was previously placed in another family, but it didn't work out. Her foster parents had found her too difficult to handle.

Since Fanny has lived with us, we have built her up from the very low place she was

in when she was placed with us. We made sure that the whole family responded to Fanny in a positive manner, praising her for her achievements and building her up with comments, such as "Wow, you look really nice today," or "The outfit you have chosen suits you really well." It was important to gain Fanny's trust, knowing that she had been let down by many people like us before.

Fanny's biggest problem was that she had frequent vicious meltdowns. She would blow up at anything that upset her. During her attack she would lay kicking and screaming on the floor, and she would keep on pinching herself and anyone who happened to be around. If any of us tried to interfere, it only made things worse. If she was safe, we would just let her carry on until she finally stopped out of mere exhaustion.

When I learned about the skills approach in a weekend seminar I attended, I couldn't wait to get home and give it a go. I called Fanny in and told her that I had had a wonderful day. "I'm the best, because you can't have had a brilliant day like me," I said to her, knowing from previous experience how she would respond.

"Loser, mine was better than yours!" she said as I expected and then went on to tell me about her great day.

I told Fanny about the skills approach that I had learned during the weekend and told her some examples of how children had overcome behaviour problems by learning skills. I had a clear idea of what skill I wanted her to learn; according to my understanding, if she was to avoid her meltdowns, she needed to learn to talk about her feelings, to tell us why she was upset so that we could help her find a better way to cope with her disappointment.

I explained to Fanny what skill I thought she needed to learn: the skill of talking to someone when she was upset to let them know how she felt about what happened. I explained to her that when I got confused, or something happened that I didn't like, I too needed to talk to someone. She appeared to understand. After all, the meltdowns were exhausting for her and a nuisance for everyone else in the family. Fanny agreed with me that talking to someone would be a better thing to do than to have a meltdown.

We talked for a while about the benefits of learning the skill. She would avoid getting upset and exhausted and we would all be happier in the house. In addition, we would be able to go to some interesting places that we hadn't dared to take her before.

I asked Fanny to give a name to the skill, but she couldn't think of anything. When I asked her to describe what went on inside of her just before she became upset, she explained that there was a whirring feeling in her head. We tried together to find a name for her skill and eventually decided it would be called "the Whirring Skill."

As her power creature Fanny wanted to have the Mask, a character from one of her all-time favourite movies by the same name. She explained that when the main character, played by Jim Carrey, put on the mask, he whirred around and while he was whirring, he was indestructible and able to do just about anything. I was impressed by her creative thinking.

As her supporters Fanny wanted to name me, her mother, and her two older sisters. She explained that as this was her first attempt using the skills approach, she didn't want too many people to know about it.

Our whole family supported her. All of us told her that we knew she could do it and reminded her of how much progress she had made whilst living with us and of the many things she was now able to do that she never thought she could do before.

Fanny liked the idea that there would be a celebration when she had learned the skill. She wanted it to happen at McDonald's with her circle of supporters. I tried to suggest to her something less fancy, such as her supporters playing Xbox with for half an hour, but she didn't buy my suggestion. "Dad, this is my first skill. We must celebrate it properly."

We then went on to role-play various scenarios where she would become upset and then respond by coming to me to tell me that her head was whirring. Fanny's mother joined us and made a video recording of us doing the role-play. I did something to upset her, and she pretended to be upset. She then said "Mask," and whirred around as she went to her mother to tell her that I was trying to upset her, and she didn't like it. I would then say, "I'm sorry for upsetting you." That's how the scenario played out.

We tried to make sure to repeat a version of the role-play a couple of times a week. Fortunately, Fanny found our role-play hilarious, and we were sure to praise her for how good she was at expressing herself with words to avoid meltdowns. Practising the skill in this way was fun for the entire family; listening to half an hour of a chid screaming and shouting had been replaced with laughter and fun.

When I asked Fanny how she wanted us to remind her of the Whirring Skill if any of us felt she needed to be reminded of it, she came up with a creative solution. "You can just ask me, "Where's the Mask?"" and needless to say, in order for us to be able to do it in the right way, she had us watch *The Mask* more than once.

We made an agreement with Fanny that if she managed to use her new skill for 4 weeks, we would celebrate by going together with her to McDonald's.

Fanny enjoyed the skills approach. In fact, she enjoyed it so much that she had trouble staying on task because she was constantly getting ideas of what other skills she wanted to start learning using the same approach.

Over the years a great many experts and experienced people had tried to help Fanny but this was the first time anyone had tried to do it by replacing her problem with a skill that she could learn. The approach had a massive impact on this little girl who, for most of her life, had been described by other people as problematic, disturbed, or naughty. Next year, when Fanny was in 6th grade at school, she became a mentor for some younger children in the third grade who needed support in learning the Whirring Skill.

Gaming addiction, 14-year-old boy

Simon had been a successful student at school, but during the last semester his grades had dropped, he had neglected his personal hygiene, and he had started to sleep restlessly. His mother had heard him scream in his sleep, "Kill them, kill them!" There was a reason for his deterioration: He had become severely addicted to a popular online first-person shooter video game. There had been many arguments about his gaming at home. Once when his mother had threatened to pull the plug from his computer, he had become furious and threatened to attack her if she would even lay a finger on any of the computer cords.

His mother reserved an appointment with their family doctor to go and talk with her about the thorny situation together with Simon. As soon as she had briefly explained the situation to the family doctor, she turned to him and asked him questions about the video game that he played. "What kind of a game is it?" "Are you good at it?" "How did you become so good at it?" "Do you play by yourself, or do you have a team online?" "What fascinates you about the game?" "Can you show me some pictures of scenes of the game?" The family doctor showed that she was interested in both his mother's concerns and Simon's fascination with the game.

As the meeting was nearing its end, the doctor began to wonder aloud what skill Simon would perhaps need to develop in order for the arguments about his playing to subside and for peace to return to the family. Because none of them were able to come up with a suggestion, the doctor suggested to the mother and Simon that they would reserve another appointment with her in two weeks to continue the conversation. She also gave both a homework assignment. To the mother she said, "I want you to talk with your husband and to think about what skill you would want Simon to learn that would help you put an end to the arguments about playing." Then she turned to Simon and said, "I have a homework assignment for you too, Simon. Your parents will be thinking about what skill they want you to learn, and your job is to give a name to that skill. I will look forward to seeing you again in two weeks and I am already curious to find out what you will come up with."

When Simon and his mother came back in two weeks, they both appeared to be in a good mood compared to how they had looked when they came in the previous time. Simon's mother reported that there had been fewer arguments about playing and that Simon had devoted a little bit more time to his schoolwork.

"Did you talk with your husband about what skill you would want Simon to learn?" the doctor asked the mother.

"We thought about it and came to the conclusion that while getting him to stop playing his video game is unrealistic, he should learn to take longer breaks from playing. For example, he should be able to put the game aside when he does his homework or when he sits with us at the dinner table."

"That sounds like a good idea to me," said the doctor. "What about you, Simon? Did you do your homework? Have you found a name for the skill your parents would want you to develop?"

"I have", said Simon. "The name of that skill is "formatting.""

The conversations with the family doctor helped to initiate a project that had positive effects not only on Simon's gaming addiction, but also on the rest of the family's screen time use as well. When his mother and Simon came to talk to the family doctor the third time, the doctor suggested that the family might perhaps celebrate in some way the positive changes that had been accomplished.

Simon said, "We can celebrate, but not until my brother has also learned the same skill that I have learned."

* * *

I hope that you have been inspired by the case stories that I have presented in this chapter and that you feel ready to check out the next chapter in which I address, in alphabetical order, all common children's challenges from A to Z.

Photo by Samu Lopez on Unsplash

7

CHILDREN'S CHALLENGES FROM A TO Z

···

A good tool is good for many purposes.

DOI: 10.4324/9781003435723-7

In this chapter you will find an alphabetical listing of common – and also some not so common – children's challenges and problems and my suggestion for how to understand and tackle them using the skills approach.

Attention deficit disorder

Attention Deficit Hyperactivity Disorder, or ADHD, is not a bodily illness or brain disorder that can be detected with laboratory tests or brain scans. Rather the term refers to a syndrome, a compilation of behavioural problems including difficulties in concentration, impulse control, and planning, coupled with fidgeting and hyperactivity. The diagnosis is a double-edged sword; it has both positive and negative consequences. Positive consequences include:

- It reduces parents' possible feelings of guilt over the child's problems,
- The child may get more understanding and assistance at school,
- The child can be prescribed stimulant medication, which may improve their attention span and reduce their impulsivity in the short-term,
- The child may feel better about themselves by thinking that there is a legitimate medical cause for their difficulties.

Negative consequences include:

- Stimulant medication has side effects and contrary to common belief is not beneficial in the long-term,
- The diagnosis and the resulting stimulant medication reduce parents' and educators' interest in developing and trying out non-drug methods to help the child,
- The child adopts the false belief that there is something wrong with their brain and that it is impossible for them to learn to control their own behaviour,
- The child's parents become dependent on experts for help.

If you want to support your child with the ADHD diagnosis in a way that is consistent with the skills approach, ignore the diagnosis and focus on your child's difficulties instead. List your child's difficulties on a piece of paper, regard them as separate problems unrelated to each other, and convert each of them, one by one, into a skill your child can improve.

In other words, help your child with an ADHD diagnosis in exactly the same way you would help them if they hadn't been given the ADHD diagnosis. Talk to your child about which skills they would benefit from getting better at to make their life easier and to be more successful at school and hobbies alike.

When you embark on a skill that your child is interested in learning – say, learning to accept failure or to keep their room tidy – help your child start a project to develop that skill.

Children with an ADHD diagnosis usually have several challenges, which means that they have room for improvement with several skills. When children have many skills they would need to become better at, it is smart to allow the more challenging skills to stay on the waiting list and start with a skill on the easy end of the continuum, a skill that your child is motivated to learn and likely to improve quickly. Once your child has succeeded at learning one skill, it is likely that they will be interested in learning more skills that are beneficial for them.

To learn more about using the skills-based approach with children diagnosed with ADHD, read the stories of 8-year-old Adam and the 12-year-olds Walter and Sara in the previous chapter.

Bipolar disorder

Bipolar disorder, previously known as manic depressive illness, used to be a diagnosis that was only given to adults, never to children. The idea that children could also be diagnosed as suffering from manic depressive illness was originally introduced in 1969 in Sweden, but the real breakthrough in applying this diagnosis to children took place in the USA in 1995 with the publication of the article "Paediatric-Onset Bipolar Disorder: A Neglected Clinical and Public Health Problem."

Childhood bipolar disorder, or paediatric bipolar disorder (PBD), is a highly disputed diagnosis. In the USA, where child psychiatry is very drug-focused, the number of children given this diagnosis has skyrocketed during the past few decades and nowadays, it is not uncommon in the US even for toddlers to be given this diagnosis.

European child psychiatrists have been much more cautious in giving this diagnosis to children. In the USA there have been attempts to halt the overuse of the diagnosis and the consequential medicating of children. The PBD diagnosis has been removed from DSM-5, the official classification system of psychiatric problems, and doctors have been guided to label children with other diagnoses instead. A popular replacement label is the newly added term *disruptive mood dysregulation disorder*.

The main reason why PBD is controversial is because its definition is so broad and vague that practically any child with swift mood changes or frequent tantrums can be given this diagnosis. According to critics, the PBD diagnosis is nothing but a label that has been invented from scratch and marketed with massive input from the pharmaceutical industry, a label that is used to justify the prescribing of psychosis medication and other strong psychopharmaceutical drugs to children.

Whether your child has been given this dubious diagnosis or not, you can help them improve their ability to control their intense emotions with the skills approach. The PBD diagnosis does not tell us what specific challenges the child has, but it can safely be assumed that a child who has been given this diagnosis suffers from swift changes of mood and tantrums. These are problems that can be tackled with the skills approach regardless of whether the child has been given the PBD diagnosis or not.

If your child suffers from tantrums, you may want to start by helping them overcome that challenge first. You can find instructions on how to tackle tantrums in this chapter under the heading "Tantrums." Once your child has gained control over their tantrums, he or she will probably be interested and motivated to use the same method to also get some control over their mood swings.

Biting

By "biting here," I am referring to a situation where a child who is over 3 years of age unexpectedly bites, pinches, or hits other individuals – whether they are children or adults – without any apparent reason.

The child's behaviour is perplexing because there seems to be no reason for it, and it's not associated with any kind of anger or aggression.

Years ago, when a good friend of mine consulted me because of her 2-year-old son's persistent biting behaviour, I did some research on this topic and bumped into an interesting approach to dealing with the problem of biting. The approach was proposed by proponents of Adlerian child-rearing, an approach to parenting based on the theories of the Austrian psychiatrist Alfred Adler that has been one of the inspirations for the development of the skills approach presented in this book.

In that approach the parent tells the biting child, "Oh, I see, you want to play the biting game?" When the child says "yes," the parent starts to play a game with the child where the parent asks the child to bite them very gently on the arm. Then the parent returns the bite and bites the child in the arm as gently as the child bit them. Next the parent asks the child to bite them again but this time just a little bit harder, and again the parent returns the biting just a little bit harder. The game continues with increasingly harder biting until the biting hurts the child so much that he or she no longer wants to continue the game. With the help of this biting game the child quickly realizes that biting hurts and that the game is not fun at all. It should be emphasised that the biting game is meant to be a game, not a way of punishing the child. The aim of the biting game is to give the child an opportunity to learn how biting feels and how it influences people without reprimanding them or telling them off.

The following story offers another interesting approach to biting problems. A 5-year-old child had a strange habit of shoving other children with his extended arms with the result that they would trip over, start to cry, and sometimes also hurt themselves. The boy appeared to get some sort of naughty satisfaction from scaring others in this way.

Needless to say, conventional ways to try to stop him from shoving others – scolding him, reasoning with him, and informing his parents – had been to no avail. Finally, one of the boy's teachers came up with a creative idea. She talked to the boy and proposed that he try another way of scaring his peers. Instead of shoving them, he could try and see what happened if he scared them in a different way, by going close to them and clapping his hands forcefully right in front of them. To the teacher's surprise the boy was delighted with the idea and began to do so. The clapping was also a bad habit, but it was not as bad as the shoving habit and his victims responded quite differently to it. The boy used the clapping habit for a few days, but soon grew tired of it and stopped doing it. He also didn't go back to his old shoving habit. I think it is interesting that the boy would not comply with the adults' attempts to get him to stop his bad habit, but he was willing to comply with the proposal to replace his bad habit with another habit, a less disturbing habit, that he was able to abandon at will.

Bullying

Your child bullies other children

What skills are missing from a child who bullies other children? One often hears people say that a child who is mean to others lacks empathy or the ability to put oneself in the other person's shoes. But empathy is a broad concept which consists of many skills, such as the skill of defending one's friends when they get bullied, and the skill of apologising when one has hurt someone else's feelings.

The skill of sticking up for friends is an essential element of empathy. You can open a conversation about the topic with your child, for example, by asking them: "What can you say, or do, if you see a child bullying another child and calling them stupid or fat?" A question such as that one can prompt a useful discussion between you and your child. The skill of sticking up for friends is a topic that children find interesting, and also a skill that they can practise with the help of role-play. "How would you stick up for me if I was a child and you saw someone else calling me stupid? Let's pretend that I'm the one who called the other child stupid. What will you say to me?" The better your child understands how important it is to protect others, the less likely it is that they will themselves engage in bullying.

Another skill that reduces bullying is the skill of apologising. It is a skill that we can help our children to learn. Children can practise the noble skill of apologising by verbally apologising for their rude behaviour to another child but also by writing apology emails, postcards, or instant messages.

Unfortunately, many parents and educators often respond to a child's wrongdoing by demanding, or forcing, the child to apologise to the child they have hurt. However, forcing children to apologise is not a good way to teach them the difference between right and wrong. If your child apologises because you demand they do so, they may comply and do what you tell them to do, but they will not learn to apologise in a genuine way. It makes more sense to say to your child something along the lines of, "I think you should apologise to Jack. You don't have to do it right away. You can do it when you feel ready. Have you thought about what would be a good way to apologise to him? Did you want to call him and talk to him, or would you rather send him a message apologising for what you did?"

Find out more about this topic at https://www.kidsskills.org/english/ responsibility. *You can also find an app that I have created that helps the users of the app to compose well-formed and convincing apology letters.*

Other children bully your child

When parents find out that their child is being verbally bullied in day care or school, they usually respond with a strong desire to defend their child. They contact the teacher, expecting the problem to be taken seriously, and that the teacher will make sure the bullying ceases. Often this works but unfortunately, in many cases, the bullying continues despite the teacher's efforts to stop it, or the bullying becomes so inconspicuous that it goes undetectable. Sometimes the bullying does cease, but the child is so sensitised to bullying that they feel bullied even if all children assert that it is no longer taking place.

For reasons such as these, it is good to know that it is also possible to approach bullying from another direction by trying to help the child become stronger, more resilient, and less vulnerable to the hurtful words of other children.

To help your child develop resilience, talk to them about what would be a wise way to respond in situations where another child says something hurtful to them. "If someone says to you that you are stupid, or something like that, what can you say back to him or her? What would be a wise way to handle the situation?" Would you want your child to counter meanness with meanness, or would you prefer them to learn to ignore the hostile words of other children?

There's one more option for you to consider. An additional alternative is to help your child learn the skill of responding to verbal bullying with wit or humour. It means that the child is able to respond to verbal bullying by saying something smart, funny, or witty, and something that breaks the cycle of meanness without anyone losing face. I imagine that in the olden days, parents and grandparents prepared their children for verbal bullying by teaching them various witty comebacks to use in challenging situations.

If you want your child to learn to respond to verbal bullying with smart humour, start by asking your child to tell you what hurtful things other children have said to them or they have heard other children say to someone else and start wondering, together with your child, what would be a smart and witty way to respond to those examples.

"What could you say back to a child who says that you are stupid?"

"I could say that he must be even more stupid, because one has to be stupid oneself to call other people stupid."

"That's quite a good comeback. What else could you say? Shall we invent some more such comebacks? What do you think would happen if you said something like, 'It takes one to know one,' or 'My mother says the same and thinks it's genetic from my father's side.'"

Your child may not find your suggestions appealing, but he or she will nevertheless get the message: Responding to bullying with humour and wit works better than trying to hurt the bully with an even nastier comeback.

A mother once told me that her teenage daughter informed her one day that she would not go to school anymore. "Why on Earth?" asked the mother in bewilderment, because the girl was a good student and had always liked going to school. Slowly the mother learned that there was a boy in the daughter's class who was harassing her by calling her "puffed-up." The mother had studied solution-focused psychology and she wanted to help her daughter find a smart and resilient way to respond to the boy. She made one proposal after the other, but the girl rejected them all.

"Ach, you don't get it," she said, "I cannot say anything like that. It would only make things worse." The attempt to help her daughter find a smart way of responding to the boy didn't lead to the desired outcome. However, just a week later the girl said to her mother during dinner, "Oh, by the way, that boy who I told you about - he has ceased calling me "puffed-up.""

"I'm happy to hear that. How did you do it? What did you say to him that made him stop?" the mother wanted to know, hoping perhaps that her daughter had used one of her suggestions after all.

"I just looked him in the eye and said to him, "Justify!" He was speechless and hasn't called me puffed-up ever since," the girl explained with a proud look on her face.

Inventing humorous responses to mean things that other people tell you is a game that children can play together with their parents. It is not always easy to come up with funny responses but just playing the game, even if the child would never use any of the invented comebacks in real-life, already serves to make the child stronger and more resilient. A smart response to another child's mean comment will work in real-life situations even if the child doesn't say anything but only thinks about the response silently in his or her mind.

Hint: If your child happens to have a superhero that they look up to, you can help them invent smart responses by asking them to imagine what their superhero would say in response to such bullying.

You can practise the art of smart comebacks with your child with the help of Witty Winny, an app that I have created for that purpose. Find it at www .kidsskills.org/bully-en

Concentration

Concentration is a broad skill that is a combination of several more specific subskills. It can be compared to the skill of driving a car.

Driving a car is not a single skill but made up of a combination of several more specific skills such as the skill of turning the engine on, accelerating and braking, steering the vehicle, parking into a space, keeping an eye on the traffic, knowing all the traffic rules and so on. To learn to drive a car, one needs to learn quite a few more specific subskills. The same is true for concentration. To learn to concentrate, one needs to learn several more specific skills that together make up the broad skill we call concentration. Examples of such more specific skills or subskills include:

1. *Ability to stay on task*
   The skill of continuing doing something challenging even if you feel like stopping.
2. *Ability to accept failure*
   The skill of tolerating failure and mistakes and understanding that it is impossible for any human being to succeed every time.
3. *Ability to ask for help*
   The skill of turning to a friend or an adult and saying, "Can you help me?" when you struggle with something, and you need another person to give you a hand.
4. *Ability to accept help*
   The skill of allowing another person to help you when they see that you are in need of some help or assistance.
5. *Ability to take breaks*
   The skill of noticing when you need a break because you are getting tired and starting to lose your concentration.
6. *Ability to make plans and stick to them*
   The skill of planning your daily activities and acting systematically according to your plans.
7. *Ability to feel proud of one's accomplishments*
   The skill of being happy about things you have done and skills you have learned.
8. *Ability to ignore distractions*
   The skill of getting immersed in an activity to the extent that you no longer pay too much attention to distractions such as sounds and other people moving about.

If you want to help your child become better able to concentrate, start by thinking about which more specific subskill your child needs to improve and help your child develop one subskill at a time.

To learn more about this topic, read the story of 9-year-old Tom in the previous chapter and read the text under the heading 'Attention deficit disorder' in this chapter.

Confabulation

Confabulation here means that a school-aged child tells other children – sometimes also adults –stories that they have made up as if the stories were true. Such stories are typically dramatic and apparently the aim of the child who is confabulating is to trigger emotional responses such as awe, sympathy, pity, or admiration in the targets.

A child's confabulation raises curiosity in people around the child. It begs the question, *what on Earth drives a child to invent stories and to try to make people believe the stories are true?* It may be difficult to find an unambiguous answer to that question. Instead of trying to find an answer to the why-question, it may be more useful to ask what skill the child needs to learn to naturally stop the confabulating. It could be, for example, "ability to stick to the truth" or "skill to be clear about which of the stories one tells other people are true and which ones are made up."

In fact, making a distinction between fact and fiction is a skill that all children have to learn as they grow up. If a child who has already reached school age has not yet learned to draw a line between fantasy and descriptions of reality, it is time for them to acquire that skill.

Making a clear distinction between fact and fiction is a skill that children can intentionally learn. It is a skill that can be practised in many ways, for example, by playing a game in which participants take turns to tell a story while others try to find out if the story is true or not. One version of this game has been on TV, where each participant tells three stories and the other contestants try to figure out which of the stories are true and which ones are fiction using questions that the storyteller is only allowed to answer "yes" or "no."

Assuming that the child who has engaged in confabulation accepts the idea that it is time for them to learn to make a clear distinction between fact and fiction, one important next step is to ensure that the child has a wide support network of people who want to help them learn the skill.

"If we, who are supporting you, become suspicious that the story that you have told is not true, then what do you want us to tell you? Would it be a good idea that in those situations we ask you, "fact or fiction?" or "true or false?", or would you prefer us to show you a sign of some sort that means the same?"

And then: "How will you answer us in case the story you have told is true? What about in the case it is a story that you have made up, how will you answer us in that case?"

It is possible to respond to a child who engages in confabulation in a similar manner that many parents respond to lying; you scold the child and possibly threaten the child with consequences if they don't stop doing it. But you can also approach the issue with the skills perspective, in which case you would not scold or reprimand the child, but you would instead support the child and help them develop skills that automatically lead to the cessation of telling fictional stories as if they were true stories.

Cursing

Cursing means here that the child causes resentment in adults by using culturally reprehensible words and expressions, or swearwords, in their speech.

When you use the skills approach to intervene in cursing, rather than asking why the child curses or what the child wants to accomplish by swearing, you focus on finding a skill that the child needs to learn to stop cursing – regardless of why he does it.

It is easier for children to stop cursing if, instead of asking them to stop cursing, you ask them to replace all the swearwords they use with some other, nicer, less disturbing words or expressions.

Have a discussion with your child about cursing and work out jointly a list of inventive replacement words for all the swearwords that they use. The f-word, for example, can be replaced with the word "frack" or "freaking," "poo" with the word "phooey," "son of a bitch with "son of a gun," etc. I am sure you get the drill. Propose to your child that they start to use the nicer replacement instead of swearwords and create, together with your child, a project to encourage and motivate them to learn that skill.

I am sure there are many more ways to help children grow out of the habit of using swearwords. I once met a kindergarten teacher who told me, with a pinch of pride in her voice, that at their kindergarten swearing had never been a problem. When I asked her what strategy they used to deal with it, she told me that they have a leather purse secured tightly with a lace hanging on the wall. If any of the children happen to release a swearword from their mouth, the teacher takes the leather purse from where it hangs on the wall, unties the lace, opens the mouth of the purse, places the purse next to the child's mouth and asks the child to repeat the swearword so that it can be caught into the purse where it belongs. When the swearword securely in the purse, the teacher ties the lace tightly and the purse is returned to its own place on the wall.

Read the story of 8-year-old Adam in the previous chapter.

Defiance

I once read an article written by a teacher concerning the obnoxious behaviour of today's students in schools. In the article she gave some examples of reprehensible behaviour that she has witnessed. This is one of the examples she described: "Many of the teachers had told Jack to remove his cap, but he didn't do a thing. He just touched his cap defiantly but didn't take it off his head. I told him that if he didn't take his cap off, I would take it off him. Since he didn't take off his cap, I took it off him. He followed me, leaning his head on me. I told him not to lean on me. He didn't stop but shoved me and said: 'Give me the f---ing hat.' I started to drag him to the teachers' room. He resisted by grabbing my legs and trying to lift me into the air. We both fell on the floor, and he didn't let go of me until the other teachers intervened. Once he was pulled off me, he hit me in the face with the palm of his hand."

All children are sometimes defiant, but if a child is defiant all the time, has a pervasive negative attitude towards everything, and constantly pushes the parents' and teachers' buttons, psychiatrists have a scientific sounding name for such behaviour: They call it ODD, or Oppositional Defiant Disorder. In recent years I have noticed that another acronym, PDA, has been invented to refer to the same kind of behaviour. It comes from the words "pathological demand avoidance," and it is mainly used by people who write and talk about autism. Defiant, obstinate, in opposition, stubborn, bad attitude, bull-headed, talking back, provocativeness ... the beloved child has many names.

No-one knows why some children develop a defiant pattern of behaviour. I like to think that it is something that evolves as a result of a vicious cycle, where the manner in which parents and other adults try to influence the child's behaviour provokes defiance in the child. Some children seem to be allergic to any adults' orders or instructions – even requests presented in a friendly manner – as if they were all unfair and oppressive authoritarian commands.

Children's persistent oppositional behaviour is a huge challenge to parents and teachers alike, but I think it is helpful to understand that defiant children also suffer from their own pattern of behaviour. I think most oppositional children know that their life would be much easier if it wasn't so difficult for them to listen and to follow adults' instructions.

If your child is persistently oppositional, there are two ways you can help them become more cooperative. You can adopt a softer style of communicating your instructions to them that takes into account their aversion, or you can help your child to develop a skill that makes it easier for them to respond collaboratively to your instructions.

Let's start with what I call the softer style of communicating. It means, for example:

- You offer your child two or more alternatives, from which they can choose the one they prefer. To use the case of the boy with the cap as an example, it might sound something like this: "Do you want to take your cap off now or do you prefer to keep it on for a bit longer?" or "Do you want to take off your cap here or when you are back in class?" "Do you want to take off your cap yourself or can you think of someone you would want to do it for you?" Offering alternatives allows the control-allergic child to feel that they are in control instead of someone else controlling them.

- You present your wish as your own problem and you ask your child to help you solve it. "It is my duty to see to it that the students don't wear their caps at school. What do you suggest for me to do?" "What do you think I should do if I wanted you to follow our house rule that we don't wear caps while we are inside the school building?" When your child feels that they are helping you solve your problem, they can avoid feeling that you are bossing them around. A child who has the tendency to respond to your instructions with defiance finds it difficult or impossible to comply with your instructions if they feel that you are bossing them, but they may be quite willing to comply with your instructions when they feel that by doing so they are helping you.

- You make an agreement with the child beforehand of a gesture or code that you will use to express your wish to them. "If I sometimes have to ask you to remove your cap off your head, what sign do you want me to give you?" "How would you want me to tell you with a gesture or code of some sort that you need to remember to take the cap off your head?" Children who suffer from excessive defiance seem to be oversensitive particularly to verbal instructions. Even if verbally expressed orders are a red flag to them, for some reason various kinds of codes or mutually agreed-upon gestures and signs are easier for them to comply with.

One way to think about defiance is to view it as a sign that the child has not yet learned the skill of following the instructions of adults, a skill that children can learn and become better at and a skill that they may in fact enjoy learning.

If you want your child to learn the skill of following instructions, start by talking with them about the benefits to themselves of learning that skill. Your child may well become interested in learning a skill like following instructions if they understand that they will gain from it. Children can practise the skill in many ways. Small children like different versions of games such as Simon Says, where one person gives orders, and the others have to follow them depending on how the order has been given.

Learn more about this topic by reading the text under the heading 'Obedience' in this chapter.

Depression

During the 80s a new idea emerged in child psychiatry according to which children, not only adults, can suffer from clinical depression. If you read texts in books or on the Internet about depression in children, you will find that the experts always make the point that childhood depression differs from adult depression. Low mood and hopelessness are not necessarily the dominant features of depression in children as they are in adults. The dominant symptoms can vary and can be anything from touchiness to self-criticism, and from irritability to rapid mood swings. When one reads what experts write about childhood depression, one cannot avoid getting the impression that the concept has been so broadly defined that almost any child who suffers from psychological problems could be given this as a diagnosis.

Depression and medication go hand in hand. If a child psychiatrist attaches the diagnosis of depression to a child, it is more than likely that the child is also prescribed antidepressant medication. The amount of antidepressant prescriptions to minors has skyrocketed in the entire Western world. This trend is problematic not only because the type of medication that is used has many nasty side-effects but also because when the treatment of the child becomes centred on drugs, interest in influencing the child's quality of life fades and becomes secondary to finding the right medication and correct dosage.

Personally, I think that we should deliberately avoid applying the term depression to children and use words of ordinary language instead, such as *unhappy, down, sad, blue, hopeless,* or even *self-destructive* when that is the case. Medical terms such as depression steer our thinking towards illness, disturbance, and brain malfunction while words of ordinary language steer our thinking towards natural causes such as losses, disappointments, and painful experiences.

When I have been speaking to professionals I have often suggested, tongue-in-cheek, that instead of giving unhappy children the diagnosis of depression we should perhaps give them the diagnosis JHGH. I usually give my audience a moment to try to figure out what the unfamiliar acronym JHGH may mean before I reveal to them that it is made up of the initial letters of the words "Joy Has Gone Hiding." My self-invented JHGH-diagnosis attempts to convey the idea that something bad has probably happened to the child, or perhaps continues to happen to them, which explains why they are feeling the way they do and why they have temporarily lost their ability to enjoy life. JHGH is an alternative diagnosis that can steer all the people who care about to child to think about what would be the best way for them to help and support the child to restore their lost ability to enjoy life.

The ability to enjoy life is coded into our genes and, under normal conditions, it is an innate skill that we don't need to learn. Nevertheless, it is a skill that any of us, adult or child, can under certain conditions temporarily lose, and no matter why we have lost it, we can always discover it again with the help of other people.

Divorce

Half of all children in Western countries live in families in which the parents are separated or divorced and who therefore often have two homes, the home of the father and the home of the mother.

According to statistics, children of divorce have somewhat more problems than children of so-called intact families. That fact has been used by psychologists and other "experts" to argue that divorce is bad; that it has a negative influence on the healthy psychological growth of children. However, gradually people have begun to understand that correlation does not mean causality, that the relationship between divorce and children's well-being is complex and there are many other factors at play. Children of divorced parents may have more problems than those of parents who stay together, but rather than being caused by divorce itself, this statistical difference is caused by other factors often, but not always, related to divorce. Such factors include, among others, economic deprivation of the family, prejudice towards children of "broken families," children lacking contact with a remote parent, conflicts and animosity between divorced parents, and parents' poor parenting collaboration.

If you are separated or divorced from the other parent of your child, there are many things you can do to help your child cope successfully with the new situation. I have collected here a few pieces of advice for you:

- Help your child realise that even if it is undoubtedly stressful to switch between two homes, the arrangement often also offers various benefits to the child.
- Make sure to always talk about your co-parent in a respectful tone of voice while your child is present.
- Do whatever you can to support the contact and relationship between you and the co-parent.
- Remember that even a thin and distant contact between your child and his or her co-parent is better than no contact at all.
- If you have conflicts with your co-parent, avoid taking them into court. Use mediation instead.
- Resist the temptation to blame your co-parent for your child's possible psychological problems. Stick to the skills approach instead by helping your child find a skill to learn and by inviting your co-parent to contribute by supporting your child in learning that skill.
- If your child is in a grumpy mood when he or she returns home after having spent time with the co-parent, avoid the temptation to automatically think that the child must have had some negative experiences while staying with the co-parent. Instead, give your child time to "settle" back into your home because their bad temper is most likely caused simply by the stress of shifting from one house to the other.
- Thank your co-parent whenever possible– in your child's presence – for what he or she has done to contribute to your child's growth and well-being.
- Give your child a copy of "Happy with Two Homes," a workbook for children of divorced parents that I have created to help children cope successfully with the two homes arrangement.

Fears

All kinds of fears are common among children. Not unlike adults, children can also develop a fear of just about anything. Common fears among children include insects, animals, darkness, social situations, needles, going to the dentist, getting lost, and high places. Children can also develop fears of vomiting, blood, monsters, robbers, intoxicated people, or bad things happening to their parents. Only imagination is the limit for what things children can become afraid of.

Fears are part of life. The human brain is simply constructed in a way that allows the fear response to be triggered easily, and once the fear is borne, it tends to persist if the person doesn't deliberately do something to overcome it.

Whatever your child is afraid of, you can help them overcome their fear. The best way to help children overcome their fears is to stop talking to them about their fear and to talk, instead, of the courage that they lack and need to build (to overcome their fear).

For example, if your child is afraid of dogs, don't talk to them about fear of dogs, but about *dog courage* and what to do to build it. If your child is afraid of the dark, don't talk to them about fear of the dark, but about *darkness courage* and what to do to build it. If your child is afraid of burglars, don't talk to them about fear of burglars but about safety and about how to build feelings of safety. When talking with your child, focus on a courage that needs building instead of a fear that needs to be conquered; it is easier for your child to join you in inventing various ways to practise and develop the courage.

It is possible to use imagination to develop courage. For example, a child who is afraid that they will be teased by some of the others at school can develop their bravery by imagining that they have an invisible protective shield that makes them invulnerable. They can imagine that if they turn on the shield at school when needed, none of the mean words from the other children can hurt them.

Another way for children to use their fantasy in developing specific braveries is to imagine that they have an invisible protector – a friend, animal, superhero – on their side in situations that are scary to them. One boy who was afraid that monsters would enter his room during the night came up together with his parents with the idea of placing some sweets on the floor so that if the monsters came, they would not disturb him but would savour the sweets they found on the floor and leave to continue their nightly explorations.

Developing bravery works best when children carry it out in small steps and on their own conditions. A child who is afraid can start by practising making contact with a stuffed cuddly toy dog, then with a puppy and only gradually move on to letting bigger dogs sniff them. Likewise, a child who is afraid of spiders can start developing their spider bravery first by reading about spiders, then watching pictures of spiders, then looking at videos of spiders, and so on, until they are gradually able to make real-life acquaintances with live spiders.

For some reason it is easier for children to develop courage than to conquer fears. When you don't talk with your child about their fears but about building a particular courage, it is easier for them to talk about the subject and to invent creative means to practise and develop that courage.

Learn more about this topic by reading the story of 7-year-old Sam in the previous chapter.

Finger sucking

Finger sucking is probably one of the most common of children's bad habits. In babies it's not a problem, but when children are 3 or older, sucking fingers becomes a problem because it causes misalignment of teeth.

To get their children to stop sucking fingers, many parents tell the child to stop doing it: "Take your thumb out of your mouth," or "Don't suck your fingers!" or "You doing it again? Stop it," or "Don't you remember what the dentist said?" However, as we all know by now, telling children to stop doing something doesn't usually work and often only makes things worse.

Milton Erickson, an American psychiatrist who was influential in the 20th century and who has been an important inspiration to me, told a story of how he helped a 5-year-old boy stop sucking his thumb. The boy's parents reserved an appointment with Dr Erickson because they had been told that he was an expert in hypnosis and that he had succeeded in helping a lot of patients, including many children. The parents sat with their son in Dr Erickson's office and described the boy's problem to him. Erickson listened patiently and then turned to the boy and said something along the lines of, "It's your thumb and nobody can tell you what to do or not to do with it." He then asked to talk with the boy alone, dismissing the parents to the waiting room. Once he was alone with the boy, Erickson chatted for a while with him about this and that, his siblings, friends, and hobbies. He then asked the boy which one of his thumbs he sucked, the left or the right one. The boy showed Erickson his left thumb. "I see, you suck your left thumb," Erickson said, "What about the right one? Don't you suck your right thumb at all? Erickson wondered aloud how the boy's right thumb feels about never getting sucked on, while the left one gets so much sucking every day.

The boy was perplexed by this unexpected angle to his bad habit. He had never thought about his thumb sucking in this way, as a form of attention that should be given equally to both thumbs. Once Erickson had the boy thinking, he suggested to the boy that he should continue sucking his thumb, but to make sure, from now on, that both his thumbs get an equal amount of time of sucking. If, for example, he would suck his left thumb for one minute, he would have to suck his right thumb also for one minute. The boy subscribed to the doctor's suggestion. In the following weeks, as the boy did his best to ensure he was sucking both thumbs an equal amount of time, the task turned out to be so cumbersome that he ended up abandoning the sucking habit altogether.

This story makes the point that it's easier for people – children and adults alike – to give up bad habits if they don't focus onget- ting rid of them, but instead try to modify them. It may be impos- sible for a child to stop sucking their thumb, but they may succeed by modifying their habit first and then getting rid of the modified habit.

I once consulted a mother and her 5-year-old daughter in a train- ing event. The mother told me that she was otherwise happy with her daughter but there was one problem: The daughter sucked her fingers and the dentist had said that it was important for her to stop doing it. I asked the mother what she had done so far to get her daughter to stop. The mother said – not surprisingly – that she had told her to take her fingers out of her mouth.

"Has it helped?" I asked the mother.

"It hasn't helped at all," she said. "When I tell her to take her fingers out of her mouth, the fingers just go deeper into her mouth."

I claimed that I knew the reason why this happened. "It's because you haven't found the magic word yet," I said, "the word that works and makes the fingers come out of the mouth."

My claim gave the conversation a new direction that also allowed the girl to participate in it. "What's the magic word that helps your fingers slip out of your mouth?" I asked.

We tested many funny magic words until we found one that the girl appeared to find appealing. I happened to have my large-sized hand puppet with me, so I grabbed it and sat it on my lap. I slipped my hand into the puppet's cloth-made hand and inserted its fingers into its mouth. We then tested the magic word with my puppet and found that it worked wonders; the puppet's fingers slipped rapidly out of its mouth every time anyone said the magic word. Before we ended the consultation, I suggested to the mother to tell her husband about our search for the magic word and to involve him in a project to find the magic word that the parents could use at home to help the daughter remember to take her fingers of her mouth.

Hair pulling

Plucking hair is a persistent habit called *trichotillomania* in medical terms. The word is used to refer to plucking one's hair, eyebrows, or eyelashes.

Parents' well-meaning instructions, such as "Stop pulling your hair" or "Don't do that," are not very helpful and may, in fact, exacerbate the problem.

Professional literature on persistent habits recommends an approach, where you don't focus on stopping or getting rid of the bad habit, but, instead, you try to replace the bad habit with another habit. The rationale here is that if you succeed in replacing your bad habit with another habit, you are then more likely to be able to overcome the new replacement habit.

If your child plucks their hair, have a talk with your child to figure out what could be a suitable replacement habit for them that they could do instead of plucking their hair. Could it be something like plucking some hairy-like material or even popping bubble wrappings with fingers? Offer your child diverse alternatives and let them decide what replacement habit they want to use.

When you use the skills approach to help your child practise and adopt the new replacement habit, pay extra attention to the step of reminding. It is important that you make an agreement with the child about how you and their other supporters will remind them of the replacement habit in a kind and fun way when the child, perhaps unaware of it themselves, start plucking their hair again.

Happiness

One possible way to understand happiness is to think of it as an ability: The skill of experiencing happiness. If so, then happiness is likely to be a broad skill made up of several more specific happiness-promoting skills, such as the ability to feel gratitude, the ability to experience success, and the ability to get along well with other people. Happiness-promoting skills are skills that children can learn and become better at.

For example, if you want to help your child become better at feeling gratitude, you can ask them every evening at bedtime to tell you about a few things that they have experienced during the day that they are happy about. If you want to help your child become better at experiencing success, you can teach them to pay attention to small successes and ask them to think about how they managed to do what they did. Likewise, if you want your child to learn the skill of calming down, you can teach your child various relaxation methods such as yoga postures, breathing procedures, or mindfulness techniques.

The many skills that contribute to the experience of happiness include, among other things, helping other people and caring for animals and plants. You can promote your child's happiness by teaching your child to perform acts of kindness and talking with them about how acts of kindness influence other people and oneself.

Greeting other people in a friendly manner can sound trivial, but it too is a skill that contributes to happiness. When two people greet each other in a friendly manner – with a handshake, a hug, a high-five, or simply by showing interest in how the other person is doing – they are engaging in an activity that promotes happiness. You can practice the art of friendly greeting with your child, for example, by familiarizing them with greeting methods of other cultures, by teaching them how to give compliments, or by teaching them to show genuine interest in how they are doing.

The ability to enjoy plants, animals, and nature is also a skill that promotes positive mental health, well-being, and happiness. You can contribute to your child's ability to experience happiness by teaching them to enjoy spending time in nature, nursing plants, caring for animals, and doing other things that strengthen the innate connection between human beings and nature.

Sport, physical exercise, working out, and other forms of bodily strain contribute to well-being and happiness. You can promote your child's ability to feel happiness by offering them opportunities to exercise and move. Any form of exercise can do the trick whether it is climbing, hiking, ball games, swimming, gymnastics, dancing, cycling, or something else. It may be a good idea to teach your child to enjoy a form of exercise that you also like yourself. Team sports offer the additional benefit that they also promote learning social skills.

People derive much joy from learning skills. No matter what skill the person is learning, making progress in learning that skill generates satisfaction and joy. Encourage and support your child in learning diverse skills: speaking other languages, baking, drawing, singing, playing an instrument, coding software, making magic tricks... The list of skills that a human being can learn is truly endless.

Children love all sorts of fun; clowning around, performing, telling jokes, laughing, tickling, playing tricks, pranks, dressing up, pillow fights, etc. Laughter is the best medicine, but it is also one of the most potent ingredients of well-being. The ability to laugh and to have fun is a skill that some people seem to be born with, but it too is a skill that can be improved with practice. Think about how you could encourage your child to learn and practise the noble art of fun. It is a skill that has a life-long positive influence on people's well-being.

Optimism is an attitude that promotes happiness. Some people seem to be born optimistic, but to some perhaps limited extent, it is also a skill that can be developed. You can teach your child optimistic thinking in a playful way, for example by playing with them a fun game in which you deliberately try to view disappointments with rose-tinted glasses. The game goes like this: Whenever anything unwanted happens (say, you miss a bus or break a glass), you try to think, together with your child, what good things might possibly come out of it.

I have mentioned a few examples of happiness-promoting skills. The list is not meant to be exhaustive, but merely a source of inspiration. There are many more wellness-promoting skills such as kindness, helpfulness, good manners, ability to express one's wishes in a polite way, ability to mediate conflicts, ability to apologize... as you can see, the list goes on and on.

Homework

Most children do their homework willingly, but for some it's an uphill battle. If your child dawdles with their homework and does their best to avoid doing it, you may need to sit down with them to help them find ways that make it easier for them to manage their homework.

Start the conversation with your child by telling them that you are convinced that they would like to take better care of their homework. Show sympathy by telling your child that you understand that doing homework is not easy. All children always have better things to do than doing homework. It is natural. It is understandable to avoid doing one's homework.

Treat your child as an expert, as someone who knows how to solve the problem. Ask them, "What could help you take care of your homework better?" Your child is likely to have at least some ideas about what could help them manage their homework better.

Have a talk with your child about who could possibly help them with their homework. Would they want you to help them? If yes, in what way? How would they like other members of your family to help them? How could their grandparents help them? Could their friends or classmates assist them in some way?

Talk with your child also about practical things such as what would be a good time of day to do homework, what room or table would be a good place to study, and what position – sitting, standing, or squatting – would work for them best. If your child finds it difficult to do their homework in their own room, perhaps there is another place in or outside the home where it would be easier for them to manage their homework. If your child is uneasy sitting down, perhaps working in a standing position would work better for them.

Sometimes the best way to get your child to do their homework is to find them a "homework support person"— someone outside the family who will take on the role of helping them with their homework. This could be a somewhat older child who is willing, for some pocket money, to help your child manage their homework.

Some children benefit from taking regular breaks while doing their homework. Set the timer on your phone to go off, for example, every 10 minutes. When your child hears the alarm, it means that it's time to take a short break. During the break, your child can do something they like to do and once the break is over, they are to resume homework. Repeated breaks can provide a rhythm to the child's work and make it easier for them to do their due diligence.

If possible, find a way to make use of the fact that children prefer teaching things to others over having to learn things themselves. Can you ask your child to teach you the things they learn by doing their homework? Or could another family member, such as a grandparent, agree to be the "student" to whom the child can teach what they have learned?

Summary: If your child neglects their homework, avoid scolding them and asking them awkward questions such as "Why haven't you done your homework?" Instead, regard your child as an expert who is likely to have at least some good ideas about what could help them to manage their duty to do their homework better. Possible solutions include getting other people's support, taking breaks, finding a better time or place, and having the opportunity to teach what the child has learned to someone else.

Interrupting

With interrupting I mean here that the child doesn't have the patience to wait for their turn to speak and, instead, constantly interrupts other people when they speak. At home the child's tendency to interrupt others may not be regarded as a problem at all, but at school interrupting the teachers and also classmates is perceived as a significant problem. It disturbs teaching because at school children are supposed to be able to control their urge to blurt out their thoughts and ideas, to ask for permission to speak by raising their hand and to wait patiently until they are granted that permission.

It is common to think interrupting others is a sign of attention-seeking behaviour and that children who do so are used to being the centre of all attention at home. This may be true, but a skills approach may work better for solving the problem. To use the skills approach you will not focus on figuring out why your child interrupts others, but on what skill they are lacking that they need to be able to grow out of their interrupting habit.

Such skills include, among others:

- The skill of using facial expressions or gestures to ask for a turn to speak.
- The skill of letting another person finish what they are saying.
- The skill of waiting until the other person signals that it's your turn to speak.
- The skill of keeping in mind what you want to say until you get the chance to say it.

Listening to other people without interrupting them is an important life skill for all of us. Most children do not learn to listen to others without some guidance. If your child has the bad habit of constantly interrupting others, you can help them get rid of their bad habit and become better at listening to other people. Start by inviting your child to give the better listening skill a name, such as "taking turns" or "two-way street talking" and once you have established a name for the skill, you can go on to inventing, together with your child, fun ways to learn that skill.

An important part of learning to become better at listening is to make an agreement with your child about how you, and also other people, will remind them in a friendly way of the listening skill when they forget all about it and start interrupting again. Remember to praise your child every time they succeed in using some sort of signal to tell you they want to say something and in managing to wait patiently until they get a signal from you to go ahead. If your child finds it difficult to learn to communicate in a reciprocal fashion, you can try the "talking stick" method. The talking stick refers to the indigenous practice of conversation where only the person holding the stick is allowed to speak and the next person who wants to say something will have to ask for the stick before being allowed to speak.

Learn more about this topic by reading the story of 12-year-old Sara in the previous chapter.

Low self-esteem

Low self-esteem means that the child does not believe in their ability to succeed and feels that they are in some way inferior to others. Conversely, one can say that good self-esteem means that the child believes in their ability to succeed and feels just as good as anyone else. It is often thought that self-esteem, or self-confidence, is a relatively stable personality trait, but it is also possible to think of self-esteem as a trait that consists of skills that can be learned and developed.

These skills include:

- The skill of registering one's own successes and feeling proud of one's accomplishments.
- The skill of knowing one's strengths.
- The skill of accepting praise, responding to it by saying "thank you."
- The skill of talking about and showing one's achievements to other people.
- The skill of accepting one's mistakes and failures.
- The skill of talking in front of the class.
- The courage to ask other children to play with them.
- The skill of praising and encouraging others.

If you want to strengthen your child's self-esteem or self-confidence, think about which one of these or related skills your child has room for improvement with, and help your child develop those skills.

To learn more about this topic, read the story of 8-year-old Amanda in the previous chapter.

Nail biting

Nail biting is a common bad habit among children. Usually, parents try to intervene by telling the child to stop biting their fingernails. They say to the child, "Don't bite your nails!" or "Take your fingers out of your mouth." However, a logical instruction to stop biting does not usually help and may even make the problem worse.

It is better to approach the problem in a different way, not by trying to get the child to stop biting their nails, but by trying to get them interested in growing their nails. The goal of this approach is not stopping the bad habit, but growing nails or getting pretty nails. It is easier for the child to be motivated to make the change if you don't talk about stopping biting nails, but about growing beautiful nails.

The advantage of focusing on growing nails is that it can be done incrementally, in small steps. Your child doesn't have to try to grow all 10 nails at once. Instead, they can start by growing 1 nail, then 2, then 3, and so on. They can also decide which fingernail to grow first, and when that one nail has grown (even if the child has kept on biting the other 9 nails) the child's achievement can be celebrated in some way. One 10-year-old girl celebrated her success by varnishing her newly grown nails and gluing hearts and other stickers on them.

Once the child has succeeded in growing one nail, it is easier for them to become interested in the idea of growing more nails. The child can proceed nail by nail until, with time, they have grown all 10 nails. In one family, the parents had made an agreement with their 5-year-old son that when he had managed to grow all 10 nails, there would be a celebration for him, that he could invite his grandparents and his two best friends from kindergarten to. The celebration took place just a couple of weeks later. At the event, all the guests applauded in appreciation as the boy's mother cut all 10 of his fingernails with a pair of nail scissors. After the nails were cut, the guests were served cake and juice.

To learn more about this topic, read the story of 7-year-old Dan in the previous chapter.

Nightmares

The word nightmares means here that a child has the same unpleasant, anxiety-triggering dream that usually wakes them up crying and feeling upset. Sometimes the nightmare is triggered by a scary event that the child has experienced, but apparently nightmares can also be triggered inside the child's imagination with no connection to any real-life event.

Children can get rid of nightmares by developing a skill: the skill of influencing the content of bad dreams. You can teach your child this skill by using the same method that Nigel's grandmother used in a picture book I have written called *Nigel's Nightmare*. The book tells the story of Nigel, who suffers from a recurring nightmare. One night, when Nigel is having a sleepover at his grandmother's, he starts to cry at bedtime.

"Why are you crying?" asks Grandma.

"I am afraid I will wake up in the night again to the same nightmare, where 3 big trucks are chasing me," Nigel explains.

"Oh, so you don't know, Nigel, that there are no nightmares," says Grandma.

"But I have nightmares," Nigel protests.

"There are no nightmares," Grandma explains. "All dreams have a happy ending."

"But mine doesn't have a happy ending," Nigel insists.

"Of course not, if you wake up in the middle and you don't wait to see what happens next," says Grandma.

Together they then imagine one possible happy ending for Nigel's dream. In that version the scary trucks that are chasing Nigel stop and the friendly looking drivers step out. "Don't be afraid, Nigel," they say, "we are not here to hurt you. We came to deliver you presents."

The joint fantasy continues with the drivers inviting Nigel to enter the cargo compartment of their trucks, to look around and to pick, from all the many presents, 3 for himself. Nigel, whose passion happens to be ice-hockey, chooses an ice-hockey racket signed by one of his ice-hockey heroes, a cool looking ice-hockey helmet and a sturdy pair of ice-hockey gloves. When Nigel's head is already on the pillow, his grandma says to him, "Remember to see your dream till the ending tonight." Nigel falls asleep with a smile on his face looking forward to the dream that ends with him getting 3 presents. He sleeps through the night and in the morning cannot remember having had any dreams at all.

If your child suffers from a recurring nightmare, you can use the same method with your child that Grandma used with Nigel in the story. Explain to your child that all dreams have a happy ending and then help them visualise a happy ending to their nightmare. The rationale of the approach is to prepare the child's brain in advance – while the child is awake – to be able to turn scary dreams into pleasant ones by changing the way they end.

Obedience

To get children to obey them, or to follow their instructions, parents use many tactics. Among the most common ones are threatening with consequences ("If you don't do as I say, you will lose…") and promising rewards ("If you do as I say, you will get…") These two widely used child-rearing tactics are effective in the short run, but their problem is that the more you use them, the less effective they become. All parents wish that their children would follow their instructions without having to present threats to them or promise them rewards.

I think parents, in general, see disobedience, or refusal to follow instructions and rules, as a sign of stubbornness. It is, however, not so simple because children suffer from their disobedience themselves even if it is not apparent. When you have a candid talk with children who constantly break the rules, it often turns out that they would in fact want to learn to become better at following instructions and abiding by the rules. They know that their lives would be easier and more pleasant if they were better able to comply with the rules and instructions of adults. But for some reason they find complying more difficult than most other children.

It is possible to think of obedience as a skill that children can learn. You can discuss the topic with your child and help them to realise that learning to follow instructions will benefit them. Things will happen more smoothly, and the atmosphere of the entire family will improve when every instruction does not lead to a heated argument anymore. Help your child come up with a name for this skill (e.g., "Yes sir," or "Okey dokey," or "Copy that.") and think of a game of some sort that allows your child opportunities to practise and get used to the idea of compliance.

"Simon Says" is an example of a well-known game that can be used to practise obedience with children. In one version of the game, all players have to copy the movements of the leader, and in another they are to follow the leader's instructions only if the leader starts their orders with the words "Simon says."

There is a fun game to teach smaller children obedience. Find an old TV remote control and let your child point it towards you and to use it to control you. The child may, for example, press a button and say "squat" or "turn around" while pointing the remote control towards you. Your child will enjoy the rush they get from controlling your behaviour with this make-believe human remote control. As you probably already guessed, in the next stage of the game the roles are reversed and then it is you who controls the child's behaviour using the human remote control.

These and similar games can help children get used to the idea that it is possible to obey their parents; that is, to accept and to follow their parents' instructions without a fuss. At the same time, children can realise that obeying benefits all parties and can be fun.

OCD

Obsessive-Compulsive Disorder or "OCD" is the medical term for the problem where a person suffers from persistent and unrealistic worries or fears (obsessions), which they try to fight back with superstitious repetitive actions, or rituals (compulsions). A child may, for example, worry at bedtime that the door of the house has been left unlocked and that therefore a burglar might enter during the night. In order to overcome the fear, the child wants to make sure that the door is locked (compulsion) but soon the worry returns, and the child requires their parents to secure the door again. This cycle of unrealistic worry and securing the door again and again can be repeated many times.

Fear of germs or dirt is another common manifestation of OCD. The child fears, for example, that their hands are dirty, even though they have washed their hands carefully just minutes ago. To overcome the worry, the child washes their hands over and over again. The worries that are characteristic of OCD involve fears that something dreadful has possibly happened or that something dreadful will happen. Worries cause the child to experience intense anxiety, which in turns triggers the compulsive actions. In order to get rid of their imaginary fear, the child often demands reassurances from their parents. If the parents give in to the child's demand for reassurance, they soon find that the relief the child gets from their reassurance is only temporary.

Various OCD worries and rituals are common in children. They can appear as early as kindergarten or, more commonly, after the child has started school. Fortunately, in most cases the worries are mild and temporary, but for some unknown reason in some children the tendency to develop unrealistic worries and try to deal with them with rituals persists and begins to cause serious suffering, not only for the child but for the child's entire family.

One of the most common OCD worries is "checking" or "securing." This means that the child secures many times, for example, that the stove is not left on, that the candles have been blown out, or that the door is locked. Many children check various things more than once, but to call it OCD, the checking needs to be repetitious, and the child needs to experience intense anxiety if they don't get to do the checking. I have listed below a few more examples of obsessions and compulsions that are common in children:

- *Ordering* means that the child feels compelled to place objects in the "correct" order and cannot stop before they feel that the objects are in exactly the order the need to be. The child can, for example, feel a compelling need to place each and every cuddly toy and doll in the exact right spot and position, or to smooth out the wrinkles of the bed cover in a particular way.

- *Hoarding* means that the child collects in their home litter or other worthless objects they find in the streets or somewhere else and experiences intense anxiety if anyone tampers with their "collection."
- *Repetition* means that the child superstitiously repeats an action or actions, thinking that by doing so they can prevent some imaginary bad thing from happening. They may, for example, tap the table 3 times or repeat some specific word in their mind a given number of times to ensure that nothing bad will happen to them or to their family.
- *Fear of fateful mistakes* means that the child experiences intense anxiety because they are afraid that they have made some dreadful mistake that will have serious consequences for themselves or their family. To overcome their anxiety, the child demands constant convincing from their parents that no mistake has been made or that nothing bad will happen.

Everyone has worries and everyone sometimes has unnecessary or exaggerated worries. Fortunately, most of us have found ways to deal with our unrealistic worries and unlikely imagined worst-case scenarios. We can ignore them and shrug them off. We can let go of our anxiety triggering imaginations, but people who suffer from OCD appear to lack that ability. Their worries take hold of them and no matter how hard they try, they are not able to let go of them. Letting go, or not paying too much attention to one's dreadful premonitions, is an important skill that we all have to learn in order to be able to enjoy life.

If your child has an OCD problem, remind yourself of the fact that worries and rituals are a very common "mind bug" in children and, in most cases, the problem disappears with time on its own. If, however, the child's worries or rituals persist and cause problems for your child and the entire family, there's a good reason to try to find some means of helping your child overcome their OCD thoughts or behaviours.

The first rule of thumb for parents whose children suffer from obsessions or compulsions is that if because of their worries, the child demands all sorts of special arrangements in the home, you should do your best to resist going along with such requests. For example, if your child has a fear of germs or filth, and they demand that all the towels in the bathroom need to be changed every time anyone visits the bathroom, you should stand your ground and resist the temptation to help them by going along with their unreasonable demands. Yielding to your child's OCD generated demands helps your child's anxiety momentarily, but exacerbates their problem in the long run.

Start by inventing, together with your child, a name for their OCD problem. Your child may already have a word for their "mind bug," but if not, feel free to suggest something. In one family the child's OCD thoughts were called "silly worries" and in another one "funny fears." One boy called his OCD "my special fault" and another one spoke about "sticky thoughts" and "getting stuck." Let your child decide what they want to call their worries or rituals.

No-one knows what causes OCD-type worries and rituals, but an explanation that makes sense to the child can help them find solutions. Your child may find an explanation like this useful:

> "We all sometimes have all sorts of worries and fears, and many of them are unnecessary, even if at the moment they enter our mind, they scare us a lot. If you are patient and you just wait for a while, they will usually fade away as they become replaced with other thoughts."

You can suggest to your child the idea that the worries are caused by some sort of creature, let's say "the worry gremlin," a creature that appears out of nowhere and puts all sorts of worrisome thoughts into the heads of children. It is easier for your child to come up with strategies to ignore their worries if they can think that their getting stuck with a worry is not a fault within, but a thing caused by an imaginary creature of some sort. If your child finds this idea appealing, you can ask them to draw a picture of the imaginary creature. The child's drawing of their worry creature will help them get some distance from their problem.

Before you start inventing new means for your child to free themselves from the spell of their worries, find out what means your child has possibly already found that have been helpful to them. You should also feel free to share your personal means of coping with your own sticky worries. Explain to your child that all kinds of worries and fears constantly pop up in everyone's mind every day and that we all have to figure out ways to deal with them and let go of them so that they don't disturb us and make our lives miserable.

Supposing your child finds the idea of the imaginary worry-causing creature appealing, you can go on and start to develop together with your child strategies to resist the creature and to break free from its spell. The idea here is that the image of a worry-creature makes it easier for your child to come up with ideas for how to fight back, or resist, or overrule the creature. Your child may, for example, start to resist their worry-creature by deliberately refraining from carrying out checking rituals demanded by the creature or by deliberately ignoring the worries and fears that the creature wants them to have.

The long-term goal is to help your child learn to ignore their superstitious fears, but it is easier said than done. It makes sense to start with a more modest goal such as being able to ignore worries for a while, or to put worries on hold for progressively longer times. For example, if your child tells you at bedtime about a worry, you can write down their worry on a piece of paper and slip the paper under their pillow. Your child may be delighted to wake up in the morning to realize that the worry is gone, and it no longer bothers them.

You can find more ideas of how to help children suffering from OCD in an article I have written about the topic entitled "Brief therapy techniques for children suffering from OCD." The article can be downloaded from my website www.benfurman.com. To find the article, sign in to the "Download area" and once you have access to the area, choose "Articles to download" and find the article in the list.

I also recommend that you familiarise yourself with "Anxious Andy," one of my self-help apps designed for children. It is an experimental computer program that helps children develop their skill of letting go of unnecessary worries. You can find the app at www.kidsskills.org/ocd-eng.

Overweight

Rising childhood obesity is a major health problem worldwide. Its causes are manifold and are related, among other things, to a poor high-calorie diet, unhealthy eating habits, and a lack of physical activity. Tackling the problem of childhood obesity is not easy and getting results depends on how well the child's family participates in the project by adopting the same healthy eating habits the child is expected to adopt.

Sometimes parents may try to influence the child's eating habits by preaching, restricting, commanding, and reprimanding, but such tactics are not helpful and can aggravate the problem. It is better to try to get the child to take an interest in reducing their weight and to develop all plans and strategies in collaboration with the child.

Start the conversation with your child by making sure they know why it is important for them to lose weight and to learn to manage their weight. You may even ask a nutritionist or other health professional to talk to your child and explain the short-term and long-term benefits of weight reduction.

As soon as your child understands why weight loss is important to them, steer away from the topic of weight loss altogether. Focus, instead, in your conversations with your child solely on habits that promote *health and happiness* that they would benefit from adopting.

You can start by making a list together with your child of various health and happiness-promoting habits and once the list is ready, allow your child to decide which one of the habits on the list they want to adopt first.

Here is an example of what your list of health and happiness-promoting habits could look like:

- replacing dessert with a glass of water,
- taking the stairs instead of the lift,
- consuming moderate amounts of food at mealtimes,
- replacing milk with water,
- eating bread without spreading butter on it,

- eating vegetables or salad at every meal,
- choosing a salad at a fast-food restaurant,
- Eating slowly and calmly,
- sharing a pizza with someone else,
- eating carrots or slices of apple as a snack,
- walking to school,
- exercising regularly,
- replacing sugary drinks with plain water.

Once your child has decided which health and happiness-promoting habit they want to adopt first, help them develop a plan to adopt their chosen habit with the support of their family and friends. Once they have succeeded in adopting that habit, celebrate their success and allow them to decide which of the habits on the list they want to adopt next.

See also the text under the heading "Unhealthy diet" in this chapter.

Perfectionism

Perfectionism means that a child strives for perfection and cannot tolerate failing or not succeeding in what they do. The consequence of striving for perfection is that the child becomes frustrated, anxious or throws a tantrum whenever the thing they are doing doesn't work out as well as they think it should.

Children who strive for perfection may react strongly to situations where they do not live up to their own unreasonable expectations. In these situations, they may start to berate themselves by saying things like: "I can't do anything," "I'm stupid," "I'm dumb," or "I'll never learn this."

The skill a perfectionistic child needs to learn is the ability to accept or tolerate imperfection, to understand that no-one can always succeed and that everyone makes mistakes sometimes. The goal for a perfectionistic child is to learn to develop a more relaxed attitude towards failure, mistakes, and imperfection, and often also towards not winning in games or competitions.

The ability to take one's own failures in stride is an important life skill in which many over-demanding children have room for improvement. Fortunately, it, too, is a skill that children can intentionally learn and practice.

One way for children to learn to tolerate mistakes and failure is to learn to say out loud something self-assuring whenever they make a mistake or feel that they have failed. They might say in those situations, for example, "Never mind," "No worries," or "Win some, lose some." All languages have such phrases or expressions that are meant to help people recover quickly from mistakes and failures. What phrases do you yourself use to cope with such situations? What do you say to yourself when the cake you have baked for your distinguished guests falls? What about when someone steals an empty parking space from under your nose? Or when you come home from the shops realising that you forgot to buy what you went there for? If your child finds it hard to accept failures and mistakes, teach them to use your own favourite self-assuring phrase until it comes as naturally to them as it comes to you.

Picky eating

With picky eating, I mean that the child is very picky about what foodstuffs they agree to eat. For example, the child refuses to eat salad or vegetables, or only agrees to eat a few foods and no others. Generally, the problem subsides with time, and very rarely does it become so serious that the child's healthy growth and development is endangered. Whatever the case, a child's picky eating is a problem because it complicates meals and causes worry in the child's parents.

You can help your picky eater by to enticing them to improve their "tasting skill," or the skill of trying new tastes and new foodstuffs. Children can develop their tasting skill by playing a game, the "tasting game," which all family members can take part in.

One possible way to play the "tasting game" is that together with your child you start tasting every day at least one or two different new foodstuffs. For example, today you taste olives and pineapple, tomorrow you taste carrots and pickled cucumbers, the day after tomorrow you taste coconut and cinnamon, etc. It is possible to find ways to make the game fun. For example, I remember playing a version of such a game with my daughters when they were little. Every time we would taste a new foodstuff, with the first bite we would make exaggerated faces of disgust and say something like "Yuck, tastes awful!" Then we would take the second bite and we would again exaggerate, but this time we would make faces of delight and say something like: "Mmm, how yummy!" We could continue the game for quite some time, alternating many times with exaggerated "Yuck, tastes awful" and "Mmm, how yummy" reactions.

Tasting new tastes can, when needed, be done in very small steps. Let's say you want your child to taste a tomato and they absolutely refuse to do so: You may suggest to the child to start by tasting an imaginary tomato, for example, by eating a sandwich with slices of invisible tomato in it. You can also keep a log of all new tastes that have been tried and to reward the child in one way or the other when they have succeeded in tasting a given number of new foods.

Learn more about this topic by reading the story of 4-year-old Linda in the previous chapter.

Playing with fire

At some point in their development, many children become fascinated with fire. They want to strike matches, light candles, participate in lighting the fire in the fireplace, etc. In some children this fascination with fire is so intense that they start to play with fire when they know that it is dangerous and forbidden to do so. When the parents discover that their child has been playing with fire, they half-automatically scold the child, telling them that it is strictly forbidden for children to play with fire and often threaten the child with some punishment if the child refuses to comply with the rules.

Children playing with fire is always a serious problem, but it is particularly serious in countries where there is a high risk of forest fires because of heat and long periods of drought. One example of such a territory is Queensland, Australia. That is where they have developed a successful intervention to respond to children who have been discovered playing with fire. It is a program where a fireman who has been trained to deliver the service visits the child's home a few times to teach the child about fire safety, things such as how to check that the fire alarm works properly, how to draw up a rescue plan for the home, how to use the fire extinguisher, how to escape from a house that's on fire, etc. The brief personal training ends with the child visiting the fire station, where they get a tour of the station, the fire trucks and fire equipment. At the end of the visit, the child is awarded an impressive pin that says "Home Fire Safety Officer." After receiving this diploma, the child can participate in spreading information about fire safety to family, friends, and classmates.

The intervention program, which was developed by Queensland fire station and local psychologists to support families with a child who has been playing with fire, is a formidable example of how the skills approach can be applied to dealing with serious and potentially extremely hazardous problems.

Punishing

All children sometimes break rules and orders by doing something that is wrong or forbidden. They may, for example, steal, lie, break things, bully their classmates, act violently, curse to the teacher, etc. When children break the rules, adults usually think that it is their responsibility to reprimand and punish the child to ensure that they understand that they have done something wrong and will not do anything similar again.

However, punishing the child is not the only way to teach children to understand the difference between right and wrong. Sometimes punishing increases, rather than reduces, the child's unacceptable behaviour.

Fortunately, punishing children is not the only way to try to ensure that the child does not do the same thing again. One possibility is to use a method that I created with my colleagues that we call *Steps of Responsibility*. It means that you talk to your child about what happened, helping your child to:

1. talk frankly about what they have done,
2. understand why it was wrong to do what they did,
3. think about what would be a good way for them to apologise for what they have done,

4. think about some way they could offer to make up the wrongdoing,
5. think about how to ensure that they will never do anything similar again,
6. consider the possibility of influencing other children so that they, too, would understand to refrain from doing anything similar.

It may be useful to think that that your child doesn't break rules because they are mean, but because they lack some skill that they need to learn to keep on the right path.

For example, if your child has the bad habit of hitting other children when they get angry, you don't need to think that they are mean. Instead, you might think that they lack a skill that would allow them to avoid hitting other children. That skill might be, for example, "the skill of apologising to the child that you have hurt," or "the skill of putting your anger into words," or "the skill of calming yourself down in situations where you become angry and have the risk of starting to hit others."

You can read more about this topic by visiting the Steps of Responsibility website, www.kidsskills.org/english/responsibility *which I designed more than two decades ago for the Finnish Board of Education with funding from the European Union. On that website you will also find an app that you may find interesting that helps young people compose thoughtfully written apology letters -* www.kidsskills.org/english/responsiblity/sorry_letter

Screen time

Parents often think about how much time they should allow their children to spend on their phones. If parents don't set any limits at all for their children, they can spend hours on end on their phones. On the other hand, if the parents try to limit the time their children spend in front of screens, they may be taken by surprise when they realise how far they will go in their battle for the command of their phones. Screen time is currently one of the most popular topics of parenting conversations all over the world.

I don't have an opinion about how much screen time children should be allowed at different ages. Instead, I can remind you of some of the principles that you may want to keep in mind when you want your child to stop an activity that they find compelling.

First, it is usually easier to get the child to start doing something else than to get them to stop doing something they like a lot. For this reason, it may be smarter not to try to reduce the time that the child is allowed to spend in front of a screen but to increase the time that the child is using for preferable activities such as socialising with other children, creative play, homework, chores, sports, studying, etc. If you want your child to spend less time on their phone or playing video games and you want them to spend more time doing their homework, you may be more successful if you don't try to get your child to reduce the amount of time they spend on playing, but thinking about how to get your child to allocate more time to doing homework.

When you talk with your child, tell them that you would want them to allocate more time to homework or whatever it is that you think is important for them and show understanding. "I understand very well that you like playing video games more than you like doing your homework, but it is my duty to see to it that you take good care of your homework. What do you propose? How can we make sure that you do your homework first and start playing only after the homework is done? What can you do and how can I help you?" You should also negotiate with your child an agreement about how they want you to remind them, if needed, of the order in which you want them to learn to do these things. "Suppose I sometimes see you playing a video game and I need to remind you to finish your homework first, so how would you want me to do it? I don't want to sound bitchy. I want to do it in a nice way. What would be a nice way for me to remind you?"

One father of two children told me that in his family screen time has never been a problem. I asked him how they had solved the problem in their family. He said, "We decide about our children's use of time. They have duties and they have free time. We make sure that they do their duties and when they have free time, they can use it in whatever way they want. If they want to use all their free time playing video games and the like, that's up to them, it's none of our business. This system has worked well in our family and even if they are allowed to use devices during their free time as much as they like, they don't normally use all that time on gaming and the like."

Read the story of 14-year-old Simon in the previous chapter to learn more about how to apply the skills approach to dealing with the screen-time challenges.

Selective mutism

Selective mutism means that a child who speaks normally at home with their family members refuses to speak with anyone outside the home, in day care or at school. At the time I was specialising in psychiatry, it was thought that selective mutism was an indication of a serious underlying emotional disturbance, but these days it is more common to think that selective mutism is simply an indication that the child is suffering from a sort of social anxiety: the fear of speaking with "strangers," which in this case means anyone outside the immediate family.

The skills approach to fears is based on the idea that it is easier for children to grow a courage than to get rid of a fear. If a child is afraid of speaking with people, they can overcome their fear by working on their "talking courage."

The most important thing about growing the talking courage is, as in growing any courage, to proceed slowly with small steps. Work out, in cooperation with your child, a ladder of progress consisting of tiny steps. A first step for the child could be, for example, to manage to play a game where the child talks to strangers represented by hand puppets. The next step could perhaps be responding to a WhatsApp message or email received on the phone, then speaking just a few words with someone on the phone, and so on.

A woman who used to suffer from selective mutism as a child told me that her first significant step in developing her speaking courage was, encouraged by her parents, to say "hello" in the morning to one of her classmates.

If your child is afraid of talking with people outside the immediate family, be understanding. Remember that children can become afraid of just about anything and that diverse social fears – and selective mutism is a social fear – are very common in children and adults alike.

Support your child in overcoming their fear: Praise the child for any steps, no matter how small, that they have taken so far in developing their courage to speak; give them positive feedback for any efforts that they make; and help them to come up with games or exercises with which they can securely learn and grow – slowly but surely – their courage of talking with people.

Self-stimulation

Children realise at an early age that touching or rubbing their sex organs gives them pleasant feelings. Some children develop a habit of doing so. Boys may stimulate themselves through playing with their penis and girls, for example, by rubbing their private parts against furniture.

According to the medical view, self-stimulation, or masturbation, is not in any way harmful, but if done in public, in plain sight of other people, it is in most cultures considered inappropriate behaviour. If a child who is no longer a toddler, self-stimulates publicly, it is time for him or her to learn that giving pleasure to oneself by touching or rubbing one's private parts is a private activity that we humans are not supposed to do in public.

If your child touches or rubs themselves in public, explain to them that it is OK to do so, but that it is something that people need to learn to do when they are alone by themselves, not something you do in front of other people. There are also many other things that are not done in front of other people. Small children, for example, may sit on the potty in front of other people, but as children grow older, they learn to go to the toilet behind closed doors. There are rules in all cultures pertaining to nudity and display of affection. For example, in some countries couples are allowed to kiss in public places, while in some other cultures even just walking hand in hand on the street is considered inappropriate and unacceptable.

Sometimes children engage in self-stimulation "automatically" without being self-aware of doing it. In such cases the first step for the child to learn is to notice and to become aware of when they are doing it. The next step is to make an agreement with the child about a place in which it is okay to do it and how you, or other people, can remind him or her to use that place if needed.

When you talk about self-stimulation with your child, start by inventing, together with the child, a word to refer to touching oneself. If your child already has a name for the activity, you can choose to use his or her word. If not, you can suggest something such as "touching," "fondling," or "stroking." Explain to your child that he or she is now old enough to learn to touch their private parts in private when other people are not around.

Separation anxiety

Some children find it challenging to separate from their parents. A child may, for example, feverously resist being left in the kindergarten or school, clinging desperately to their parents. If your child finds it difficult to separate from you and you feel bad about leaving your crying child behind, you may want to try to solve the problem using the skills approach.

Separating from one's parents – or separation skill – is an important competence that every child needs to learn sooner or later. Most children learn that skill naturally and there is no need to pay any extra attention to it, but some children find it challenging and need some help and support in learning it.

Start by inventing, together with your child, a fun name for the separation skill that the child can understand. It can be, for example, "Bye-bye skill," "See-you-soon skill," or "So-long skill." If the child is small, you can start by practising the skill with a doll or cuddly toy by playing a game where the toy needs to learn to separate from the child because it is going to be taken care of for a while by grandparents or will be visiting some other place.

Such a game offers the child opportunities to find ways for their cuddly toy to succeed in staying in other care for gradually longer periods of time. The same methods become available to the child when it is time to start practising separation-skill in real life with parents. Be generous in terms of praising your child for good ideas, for trying and for making even small progress.

Shouting

Controlling the pitch and volume of one's voice is a social skill that all children need to learn. A child who speaks loudly or who shouts is probably not aware of the volume of their voice. Therefore, the first step for a child who is too loud is to learn to become aware of the volume of their own voice.

One smart way to help children become more aware of the volume of their voice is an app that can be downloaded on your phone, that shows the volume of one's voice in a visual form. Another alternative to teach children volume awareness is to use your hand for signalling. You can say, "Now you are speaking this loud," while you raise your hand to a certain level in front of you. "Say the same again with a slightly lower voice and I will use my hand to show you your volume."

When the child becomes more aware of the volume of their voice, the next step for them is to learn to control the volume in situations where they tend to speak too loudly.

An important part of helping a child learn to control the volume of their voice is to let them decide how they want other people to remind them of the skill. It is possible to find playful ways to do it. You may, for example, pretend that somewhere on your child's body there is a "volume knob" that can be turned right to raise the volume and left to lower the volume. The game prepares the child for simple gestures that you and their other supporters can use to remind them of the skill of turning down their voice when it is too loud for the situation.

Shyness

Sometimes parents worry that their child is overly shy or timid. In these situations, it is good to keep in mind that as a rule shyness and timidness is a period that lasts for some time and passes on its own accord. The less you are worried about it, the easier you make it for your child to understand that they are simply going through a natural phase of development.

Incidentally, it would not hurt if we all learned to appreciate the fact that we are all different. Some people are social, or extroverted, while others are more timid, or introverted. There's room in this world for us all. Timid people often have skills and talents that more social people don't.

Having said that, if you are worried about your child's shyness or if your child suffers from their timidness, you may want to think of some ways to encourage your child to develop their social courage.

Developing courage – any courage – works best when you take baby steps, and the child feels that they are in control of progress. What would be the first little sign for you that your child is starting to develop their social bravery? Would it be that they greet someone, or that they would talk to someone on the phone? Or would the first small sign be that your child would raise their hand in class and give a short answer to the teacher's question? If such steps seem overwhelming to the child, you can start by using hand puppets to practise social interaction. With puppets you can play out various social situations and practise safely tackling them.

Sibling rivalry

If you have more than one child in your family, you probably know from experience that siblings have a tendency to argue, fight, compete with one another, and they may even physically attack each other. Children can be nasty towards their siblings in many ways and even bullying is not uncommon.

Children seem to adapt astonishingly well to their ongoing battle with their siblings. Parents, on the other hand, tend to suffer from their children's fighting and the fact that they constantly have to intervene and try to mediate between their offspring.

The term "sibling rivalry" is often used to refer to siblings' constant arguing and quarrelling. This choice of words suggests that the problem is caused by competition and jealousy between siblings. I doubt that this explanation, regardless of whether it's true or not, helps us to find solutions to the problem.

There are other ways to make sense of the same behaviour. According to the skills approach, the constant quarrelling between siblings is caused by a lack of certain skills that the siblings have not developed *yet* — skills such as the skill to care for, or to be kind and helpful, towards each other. To think of sibling rivalry as an indication of missing skills can be useful because it is easier to help children develop desirable behaviour than to try to reduce their undesirable behaviour; in other words, it is easier to cultivate kindness, tolerance, and helpfulness than to get rid of jealousy, envy, and rivalry.

Siblings are born with an innate will and ability to help and support each other. However, their ability to be supportive of each other can sometimes become dormant if children do not have sufficient opportunities to practise and exercise it. The ability to be supportive of siblings is made up of what could be called "sibling skills," which can be developed and strengthened through exercise and practice.

To reduce sibling quarrelling, don't blame them for constantly arguing with each other, but instead focus on giving them opportunities to strengthen their sibling skills. Talk with them about sibling skills and let them participate in deciding which sibling skills they want to learn to get along better with each other and what would be a good way to learn those skills.

I've collected below some examples of skills you can help your children learn to get along better with each other:

- 'Caring skill' – ability to take care for your sibling.
- 'Kindness skill' – ability to be kind towards your sibling.
- 'Playing skill' – ability to play nicely with your sibling.
- 'Helping skill' - ability to help your sibling when they need help.
- 'Loving skill' – ability to show warm feelings towards your sibling.
- 'Thanking skill' – ability to thank your sibling when they have given you something or helped you in some way.
- 'Encouragement skill' – ability to encourage your sibling when they are learning new skills.
- 'Mentor skill' – ability to teach your sibling things patiently.

- 'Sharing skill' – ability to share toys and other things.
- 'Compromise skill' – ability to resolve conflicts on your own.

You can you help your children learn the thanking skill, for example, with the help of the following exercise. Make it a habit to discuss successes with your children at dinner. "Samuel, it's your turn to start. What you have done today that you are proud of, that you have succeeded with?" "What about you, Anton?" When your children have talked about their successes today, help them think about how they could thank each other. "We are all proud of you. Samuel. Well done. Thanks for sharing. Who contributed to your success? How did Anton contribute? What can you thank him for?" "What about you, Anton? How did Samuel contribute? What can you thank him for?"

It may not be easy at first for your children to thank each other for their own successes, but with your help they will gradually learn to thank one another for their successes – and the more they thank each other, the less they fight with each other.

Sleeping

Your child sleeps in your bed

Some children find it difficult to learn to sleep in their own room or their own bed. Parents may solve the problem by allowing the child to sleep in their bed or by making special arrangements such as one parent sleeping the night with the child in the child's room.

However, before long such special arrangements become a burden on the parents, and they are not in the best interest of the child either. It may then be time to start to think about how you can best help your child learn to fall asleep in their own bed. It is a skill that every child must learn sooner or later.

Explain to your child why you want them to learn to sleep in their own bed: "I sleep better, and you sleep better too. When I sleep better, I'm in a better mood in the morning and you, too, will wake up feeling happy. Besides, once you have learned to fall asleep in your own bed, you can invite your friends over for a sleepover and they will probably want to invite you over for a sleepover too."

Make sure other members of your family agree with you that it's time for your child to learn to sleep in their own bed. Your child will be more motivated to learn the skill if they know that this is not merely your wish, but an important skill that everyone important to them wants them to learn.

You can put a calendar in your child's room where they can put a mark on all the nights that they have successfully fallen asleep in their own bed. Once your child has accumulated a pre-agreed number of marks, it is time to celebrate the learning of the skill in the previously agreed way.

Child crawls into your bed at night

Many children wake up at some point in the night and, while half-asleep, crawl into their parents' bed to sleep the rest of the night there. Some parents welcome their child into their own bed, but others are disturbed by it, especially if the child sleeps restlessly and there is limited space in the bed.

If you want your child to learn to sleep in their own bed through the night, your child would need to learn the skill of "going back to sleep in your own bed if you wake up in the middle of the night." Explain to your child that they have now become so big, that it is time for them to learn to sleep in their own bed through the night until the morning. Help them think of a funny name for this skill and ask them to choose a cuddly toy to help them learn the skill. Also, make an agreement with the child about how many nights they should manage to sleep in their own bed till the morning before a party can be arranged to celebrate and honour the child's learning of the skill.

If you have made an agreement with your child about the number of nights they need to manage to sleep in their own bed until the morning, you can put a calendar in your child's room to mark the nights when they have managed to sleep in their own bed through the night. If sleeping in their own bed until dawn is too much of a challenge for your child, you can go slow and start by allowing your child to sleep on a mattress on the floor in your bedroom instead of allowing your child to sleep in your bed.

You can develop some sort of game with your child to help them practise falling asleep again in their own bed. For example, you could pretend that it is night-time and the child "wakes up" in their own bed in the middle of the night. When the child "wakes up," they then do something to help themselves fall asleep again. For example, they might stroke their teddy bear and whisper silently to it, "Oh, you woke up dear. It's all right. I'm here with you. I'll hold you until you go back to sleep."

See the end of the story of 8-year-old Adam in the previous chapter.

Soiling

Soiling or encopresis means that a healthy child over 4 years of age soils their pants repeatedly because they refuse to go to the toilet. The child holds on until pressure finally forces the smelly faeces into the trousers. Sometimes the problem has started with painful defecation caused by constipation, but most of the time the cause of this strange problem remains a mystery.

Professionals often think that in order to help a soiling child, it is important to find out why the child refuses to go to the toilet. This is easier said than done. The child doesn't know why they don't want to go to the toilet. Professionals have many theories, but they don't have an agreement about which is the correct one.

It may be more fruitful to ask: "What skill should the child learn so that they will no longer defecate into their trousers?" One possible answer is that they need to learn the skill of "going regularly to the toilet," or, perhaps in some cases, the "courage to go use the toilet." Whatever skill the child needs to learn, it is probably possible to find a fun and creative way to practise it.

The late Australian family therapist Michael White described in the 80s a creative way to help soiling children that became known as the "Sneaky Poo" method. White explained to the child and their parents that the child's soiling was not the fault of the parents, nor the child's own fault. It was caused by "Sneaky Poo," a nasty little creature that makes the child's faeces go to their pants. The idea is to help the child and their parents view the problem in a new light, not as a serious mental health disturbance (as they have been led to think by experts), but rather as the antics of the Sneaky Poo. Once everyone is on the same page, it becomes possible to develop a therapy programme aimed at resisting Sneaky Poo and sending it packing.

The family is invited to think about things that Sneaky Poo likes children to do, and the things that it doesn't like children to do. Usually, the family soon comes to the conclusion that one of the things Sneaky Poo doesn't like children to do is for them to go regularly to the toilet. That observation leads to the tactic of resisting Sneaky Poo by deliberately going regularly to the toilet and sitting on it for a given time.

Another way to resist Sneaky Poo includes organising the child to race with it. In the family therapy session, the therapist asks the family to draw a map of the child's home and its surroundings, and once the map is complete, the child will point to the spots on the map where Sneaky Poo usually attacks them. During the next week the family organises a race, where the child runs to the toilet from the various spots marked on the maps where Sneaky Poo has attacked the child. The idea with the race is to become quicker than Sneaky Poo. One of the parents is responsible for the child's proper racing outfit – usually the costume of the child's superhero – while the other parent is responsible for timing the child's runs on a stopwatch.

There was an interesting detail in the Sneaky Poo that caught my attention. Sometimes the family would come back for the next session and would report to White that there had been a setback; the Sneaky Poo approach had initially worked wonders, but then, after a while, the problem had returned. White dealt with these situations in a creative manner. He said, "Oh, it's my fault. I forget to tell you about tigers. When Sneaky Poo realizes that the child has had enough and is determined to send it packing, it often starts to fight back and that's when you need tigers to help you. You see, Sneaky Poo is not afraid of many things, but it is afraid of tigers." Once the children would have this additional information, they would take advantage of it. They would, for example, draw pictures of tigers, attach photos of tigers on the toilet walls or get themselves a stuffed tiger to be their special supporter. I found White's idea of recruiting tigers as helpers so clever that I have integrated this into the skills approach that I describe in this book.

The Sneaky Poo method developed by White was revolutionary. He showed beyond a doubt that even the kind of problems that are normally considered to be serious child psychiatric disturbances – and soiling is a prime example of such a problem – can be successfully treated using a playful approach where the child's parents play an active role in supporting and helping the child conquer the problem.

If your child suffers from soiling, don't pay too much attention to what the "experts" believe and use the skills approach instead. Assume that soiling is merely a sign that your child hasn't *yet* acquired the skill of going regularly to the toilet. Let your child give a name to the "toilet skill" and support them in learning the skill through deliberate practice carried out as a playful game.

If, for any reason, your child feels that sitting on the toilet regularly is too big of a step, you can help them to think of some smaller milestones. For example, your child can start the project by doing something else that Sneaky Poo would probably not like the child to do. such as learning to take care of "accidents" on their own. The child can start the skill-learning project by first learning to take off their soiled clothes after the accident, put them directly into the washing machine, wash up, and, finally, put on clean clothes – all by themselves without the help of the parents. Surely Sneaky Poo would not like them to develop skills like that!

To learn more about this subject, read the story of 5-year-old Jesse in the previous chapter on this topic.

Tantrums

When children are two, it is common that they react to disappointments with fierce tantrums — attacks consisting of crying, shouting, kicking, hitting, and smashing things. The reason for this reaction is immature development of the cortical parts of the brain. Another way to put it is to say that they lack the ability to control their anger and to regulate their emotional reaction when they become mad at something.

Normally tantrums fade by themselves when children grow older and their brains mature and become capable of handling emotions better, but in some children this development takes so long that the parents are at a loss trying to figure out what to do to get the child to stop having tantrums.

When the child is still small, the best way to help them overcome their tantrums is to not pay too much attention to the child's extreme reaction or, if possible, to take the child onto your lap and try to calm them down, for example by talking to them in a soft voice or stroking their hair. What works with small children doesn't usually work with bigger children and can, in fact, make things worse.

I was once speaking at a parent's evening at a school when at the end of the event a woman approached me and asked me if I had a few minutes of time to talk to her. She said she wanted to know whether I thought it was wrong what she did with her 6-year-old son who used to have fierce tantrums.

"So, what did you do?" I asked curiously.

"I was with him in a supermarket, and he wanted me to get him something that I didn't want to buy for him. He responded by doing what he had done many times before. He threw himself on the floor and started crying and shouting and kicking in the air unrestrainedly. I don't know what came over me, but I was so sick and tired of his tantrums, that I wasn't thinking about what I was doing. I, too, threw myself to the floor and started crying and shouting and kicking in the air, imitating him."

"Okay, and what happened?" I was keen to know.

"My son stopped his tantrum short and came to me to try to stop me: "Mom, stop it. Don't do that. I'm ashamed of you," he said to me as if I hadn't ever had to be ashamed of his tantrums."

I admired the mother's creative courage and asked her if her reaction had had a lasting effect on her son or had it perhaps only worked that one time.

"He tried to have a tantrum a few times after that, but when I noticed what was happening, I told him if he's going to have one, I'm going to have one too and that worked well."

"You asked me if I think what you did was wrong," I said. "I think you acted wisely, and I cannot imagine that what you did could in any way be detrimental to your child's development. On the contrary, he can be proud of his creative and bold mama."

To outgrow tantrums, children need to develop their self-control. It is a skill that we all need to master in our lives. We need that skill to be able to resolve conflicts with words rather than fists and firearms.

If you wish to help your child outgrow their tantrums you can start by discovering, together with your child, a word or name for their tantrums. It could be whatever sounds right to your child. Examples include fit, eruption, explosion, blast, bang, fury, blowing your top, etc. Naming the tantrum makes it easier to talk about the issue while providing a foundation for a conversation about what the child can do in the future to prevent a full-blown tantrum from being triggered.

Continue by talking to your child about what they could do (the emphasis here is on the verb "do") when they become mad that would help them calm down sufficiently to escape a tantrum: "What could you do in those situations where you become angry, that would help you cool down a bit, just enough to avoid the explosion?"

Help your child figure out some means by which they can calm themselves down in situations that aggravate them. There is a myriad of ways that children can try to calm themselves down when they are angry. They may, for example, count to ten, breathe in and out slowly 3 times, say something calming or self-soothing, stomp their foot, leave the situation, and go to talk to someone, etc. One 5-year-old boy came up with the lovely idea of what to do instead of starting to cry, shout, and hit people. When his teacher asked him what skill he needed to learn to avoid his tantrums, he answered that he needed to learn to sulk. The boy, despite his young age, appeared to have insight into the process of learning self-control; one of the first small steps in developing that skill is, indeed, to learn to sulk instead of acting out.

Once you have an agreement with the child about what they want to learn to do to calm themselves down, offer them plenty of opportunities to practise the skill. You may, for example, play a game with your child where you pretend that they are mad because of something that has happened and then they show you how they calm themselves down using their tactic. Practice makes perfect, as the saying goes.

Don't forget to agree with your child about how you, and other people, can remind them of their self-control tactic when they are in a tight spot. A mutually agreed-upon gesture or code is likely to work much better than any kind of verbal reminder.

To learn more about how to help children with tantrums, read the story of 12-year-old Fanny in the previous chapter. You may also be interested to read, together with your child, an illustrated story that I have written based on the skills approach called "Linda tames her tiger."

Tics

The word "tic" refers to repetitive involuntary movements, or twitches, usually in the region of the forehead, eyes, or mouth. Tics can also occur in shoulder regions or arms, and they can also be vocal when they resemble coughing, sniffing, or clearing one's throat.

It is common for children to have tics and in most cases the tics disappear on their own. In some children the tics persist, and this is when the parents typically consult experts with the hope of getting help for their child.

The cause of tics is unknown, but it can be assumed that the symptom is caused by some sort of disturbance in the neural pathways responsible for controlling the muscles of that particular area. Tics are not voluntary. Efforts to voluntarily control or stop the tics are not helpful and may actually exacerbate the problem.

It is possible to try to alleviate tics with medication, but the effect is very limited. Luckily tics can also be treated by teaching the child ways to control them. This method, which has been described within the cognitive-behavioural therapy movement, is known as *habit reversal training*.

If your child has a persistent tic symptom that doesn't seem to go away on its own over time, have a conversation about the tic with your child. Let your child give the tic a name that makes it easier to talk about it and encourage your child to use the mirror to see what their tic looks like. It is important for treatment to work that your child learns to talk about their tic in an open manner, not unlike stuttering children, who need to learn to talk openly about their stuttering with their speech therapist and loved ones.

When your child's tic is no longer a taboo but something that can be talked about matter-of-factly, you can try the habit reversal approach with them. Your first step can be an assessment to find out how frequently their tic appears in a given timeframe. Assessing the frequency of the tic makes it possible to keep an eye on progress and to convince the child that it is actually possible for them to gain at least some control over their tic with this form of deliberate practice.

You can also ask your child to deliberately try to increase the frequency of a tic. "Now you made 4 of them in 1 minute. Let's see if you deliberately go up to 8 tics in a minute." When the child discovers that they can intentionally increase the frequency of their tic, they can begin to think that it may be also possible for them to deliberately decrease the frequency of the tic.

Your next task is to help your child notice in advance when a tic is about to occur. This is possible because people who have tics usually have some kind of feeling, or prescience, that tells them that the tic is about to happen, not unlike how we all experience some sort of feeling that tells us just a few seconds in advance that a cough or sneeze is coming on.

This feeling, or pre-knowledge, makes it possible for the child to deliberately perform another movement right before the tic to prevent the tic from being triggered. This reversal movement should resemble in some way the tic while being less conspicuous. For example, if the child's tic involves clearing their throat, they may immediately upon becoming aware of the urge to clear their throat take a deep breath, or if the child's tic involved blinking their eyes, they may close their eyes for a brief moment just before the blinking would happen.

Children hardly notice their own tic symptoms, but parents are often unduly worried about them. It is important to understand that tics are not an indication of any underlying psychological disorder. They are just tics. They usually go away on their own and even if they don't, it can be possible for children to develop a skill that will help them gain some control of their tics.

Traumatic experiences

Parents do their best to protect their children from emotional shock experiences, but whatever they do, there is no way they can protect their children from bad things happening. At some point in their growth and development, all children inevitably experience upsetting things such as the death of a family member, being bullied by siblings or peers, witnessing a crime, seeing one's parent being intoxicated, experiencing domestic violence, sexual harassment, illness, accidents, suicide, fire, etc.

Children have an extraordinary ability to cope with upsetting experiences. They process their experiences in many ways, including simply thinking about it, drawing pictures of it, talking about it with family or friends, and playing games that allow them to process the upsetting experience on a symbolic level. Children are probably also able to process their adverse experiences in their dreams while they are asleep.

When your child has had an upsetting experience, the first thing for you to do is to remind yourself of the fact that children are born with an innate ability to cope with adverse experiences. If you still feel worried about your child's ability to cope with their experience, you can contribute to your child's recovery by observing the following guidelines:

- Avoid pushing your child to talk about their experience. Instead, offer your child opportunities to talk with you about their experience on their own initiative by spending time with them.
- If it appears to you that your child is not willing or ready to talk with you about their experience, they may, however, be willing to process their experience through drawing or listening to stories describing similar or related experiences.
- If your child wants to talk with you about their experience, listen to them without interrupting them. Do your best to answer their questions and show particular interest to things that they have done to cope with their experience.
- Praise your child for what they have acted wisely about at the time of their experience and for how they have dealt with their experience since it happened.

Children recover from almost anything, and the best way that we can support them is to simply be present and to show them that we appreciate their own unique coping strategies.

Upsetting experiences can trigger nightmares. See the section about nightmares in this chapter to find out how to help children overcome nightmares. Parents' divorce is an upsetting experience that touches in the lives of many children. See the section about divorce in this chapter to learn more about how to help children cope with divorce.

Unhealthy diet

If a child consumes excessive amounts of fatty food or food with low nutritional value such as pizza, burgers, sugary soda, and sweets, it is commonly assumed that the problem does not lie with the child but with the parents who allow this to happen. Consequentially, professionals often try to solve the problem by trying to influence the parents; giving them instructions to make sure the child sticks to a healthier diet. That is, however, easier said than done. It is a well-known fact that changing habits is difficult or next to impossible for people.

It may be a better strategy to focus on the child instead of the parents and try to help the child adopt healthier habits with the support of their parents.

If your child has an unhealthy diet, talk to them about the topic of healthier eating and tell them that you are willing to help them adopt a heathier diet. Include other adults who are caring for your child in the conversation and invite them to join forces to help the child develop healthier eating habits. It is easier for your child to modify their diet if it is not only your wish but a goal that all the important people in the child's life are supportive of.

Shy away from criticising your child for eating unhealthy foods. Instead, talk to them about why it is important for all of us to learn to develop healthier eating habits. Don't try to motivate your child by pointing out all the negative consequences of an unhealthy diet. Talk to them about the benefits of a healthy diet instead. Draw up a list, together with your child, of diverse healthy foods and nutritional habits and allow your child to decide which new eating habits they want to adopt first.

Rather than criticising your child for eating unhealthy foods, praise them whenever they eat in a healthier manner. One of the best ways to support your child is to join them in adopting healthier eating habits yourself.

Violence

With violent behaviour I mean here that a child hits, kicks, shoves, or scratches other children, or spits on them, or does something similar towards their own parents or other adults around them.

Violent behaviour is unacceptable, and it is therefore the duty of the child's parents to help the child stop their violent behaviour. Whatever the reason for the child's violent behaviour, it is important to help the child find a skill to learn that allows them to gain better control of their anger. The missing skill is, by definition, the "ability to respond to anger and frustration in a socially acceptable manner." Accordingly, one can say that a child who uses violence has not *yet* found better ways to deal with their anger, ways that they can learn and develop with the help and support of their family and friends.

Four-year-old Emmy had the bad habit of hitting other children in kindergarten. When her teacher sat down to talk to Emmy about the issue, she said to her: "I have noticed that when you get angry with the other children, you sometimes hit them. I'm sure you know that it is wrong to do so. We don't want you to hurt anyone, but I can help you. How about from now on, whenever you get angry with another child, instead of hitting anyone, you will run to me as quickly as you can, and you tell me what happened that upset you. When you have told me, I will help you find a solution. Do you want to learn to do that?" Emmy understood that it was a skill worthwhile learning.

Ten-year-old Jack attended a small alternative school where the entire staff had been trained in the skills approach. Jack had the bad habit of attacking other children when he became furious. The problem was serious because the parents of some of the other children in the school had started to voice demands that Jack needed to be excluded from the school. The principal of the school had a frank talk with Jack. "Listen Jack, you can never again attack any of the other children in our school. If we don't succeed in figuring out some way to put an end to that kind of behaviour, I will have to tell your parents that you can no longer continue to be with us. Next time you become angry, for whatever reason, you cannot attack anyone. You have to do something else instead. You must do something to help yourself calm down. What could it be? What can you do to calm yourself down?"

Jack thought for a moment and then said that it would help him if he ran to the school's respite room and banged the big cushions there with his fists.

"That could work," said the principal, and he asked Jack to show him how he would do it. Jack pretended that he was angry and ran swiftly to the respite room to bang the pillows with his fists.

"This time it worked just fine," said the principal, wondering aloud whether Jack would be able to do the same in real-life situations when he became cross with someone over something they had said or done. The principal asked Jack to show the same procedure to his teachers so that they would know what he was supposed to do to control himself next time he became angry for whatever reason. Jack practised his new behavioural response every time he showed various people – teachers, classmates and his parents – what he intended to do from now on when he became angry. The principal also made an agreement with Jack about how his teachers and his classmates would remind him of the respite room when needed. In the following weeks, Jack ran many times to the respite room to bang the cushions with his fists, but he never attacked anyone again.

A 6-year-old girl hit other children in a kindergarten. She had been told many times not to do so and she knew quite well that what she was doing was wrong. Her teacher had taught her to apologise to the children she had hit. Apologising to the victim was a skill she mastered well, but it didn't make her change her behaviour; she kept on hitting others. When the teachers wondered in a meeting what to do to help the girl stop hitting others, they came up with an idea. They thought that since apologising to the children she had hit had not had any effect, she should perhaps be required to extend her apology to the parents of the child she had hit. The teachers presented the idea to the girl's father, a single guardian, and he agreed despite the possibility that he would sometimes in the afternoon have to stay and wait for some time at the kindergarten for the parents of the child who had been hit by her daughter to show up to collect their child from the kindergarten. During the next week the girl learned to apologise for her behaviour, not only to the children she had hit but also to their parents – and probably even more importantly, her father now witnessed her doing so. This small, but apparently significant change in the way the girl presented her apology yielded the desired outcome in just two weeks.

The skill of apologising is one of the skills that help children stop their violent behaviour, but for the apology to work it is important that you talk to your child and help them think of what would be a good and befitting way to present the apology for it to have the desired effect – not only on the victim but on the perpetrator as well.

Self-control – or anger management – is a skill that all children need to learn. Small children are not yet capable of controlling or regulating their emotions. When they become disappointed, they cry, scream, hit, fight, kick, etc. As children grow older, they learn to regulate their emotions and to control their anger. Instead of acting violently, they learn to respond to anger in more mature ways, such as by expressing their anger in words, going over to talk to an adult, or by doing something else that helps them avoid behaving violently. If it is difficult for a child to learn these skills for one reason or another, work with the child to think about which self-control skill they should learn and help them to learn it. If for any reason it is difficult for your child to learn those skills, talk to the child to figure out together with them what skill they need to learn to gain better control of their anger and help your child make a plan to learn that skill.

You can find more information on the topic of apology in the section with the heading 'Punishment' in this chapter.

Wetting

Daytime wetting

Daytime wetting, or "diurnal enuresis" as it is called in medical lingo, means that an otherwise healthy child who, judging by their age, should already have learned to be continent, wets their pants at least once, but often several times a day.

If you try to handle the problem by letting your child use a diaper during the day, the process of learning to be dry may become prolonged. It may be better to figure out what skill the child needs to learn in order not to wet their pants during the day.

In one daycare centre there was a 3-year-old hyperactive boy who wet his trousers daily, and on some days several times a day. According to the staff the boy was so hyperactive that he simply didn't have the patience to take a break from his activities to go to the toilet to void his bladder. When the staff sat down to think about what skill the boy needed to learn, they concluded that the boy needed to learn "to stop every once in a while, and to listen to his body;" in other words, to stop and stand still for a few seconds to feel whether he had the urge to pee or not. If he would feel that he needed to go, even just a little, he would have to go and if he would feel that he didn't have the urge, he could pass and keep on doing whatever it was that he was doing.

One of the staff explained to the boy what skill he needed to learn to avoid wetting his pants and suggested to him that a few times during the day she would give him a sign that meant that he should stop and listen to his body, to feel whether he had an urge or not. The boy understood the idea and a game was developed to help him acquire the skill. In the game the boy was to walk into the toilet upon getting the sign from the staff and to stop in front of the porcelain toilet seat and then ask the seat. "Do you need my pee?" Once he had posed that question to the toilet seat, he was supposed to wait to hear what the toilet seat answered. If it said, "No, I don't need your pee right now," the boy was to return to his games, but if the toilet seat answered. "Yes please, I need some of your pee," then the boy was to open his trousers and give his reservoir of pee to the toilet. The boy was fascinated with the game and quickly learned to develop control of his bladder.

A grandmother told me that she had succeeded in teaching her granddaughter to become dry while she took care of the girl during the time the parents were on holiday for a week. The grandmother had wetted the groin of a doll and said to the girl, "Look darling, this doll has wetted herself. Shall we teach it to use the potty?" The girl readily agreed and the two of them joined forces to teach the doll the skill of sitting on the potty. "How can the doll notice that she needs to go?" "What should the doll do when she notices that she has the urge?" "How long should the doll sit on the potty?" "How should the doll be wiped after having been on the potty?" Step by step, as the doll acquired the skills of using the potty, the girl, too, acquired the same skill. When the parents returned from their holiday trip, the girl proudly told them that she no longer needed to use the diaper during the day because she had learned to use the potty instead.

Read the story of 6-year-old Sunny in the previous chapter.

Bedwetting

Bedwetting means that the child urinates in his or her bed while asleep even though the child is already old enough to be expected to be dry throughout the night. Learning to be dry throughout the night is a physiological skill that children usually learn by the age of 3 or 4, but for some children – for an unknown reason – it takes years to develop that skill. Fortunately, keeping dry throughout the night is a skill that children can deliberately practise and learn.

The rule of thumb in helping children who suffer from bedwetting is not to focus on reducing wetting, but on increasing dry nights instead. You can place a calendar on the wall of the child's room and use it to make a mark on each day the bed is dry in the morning. You can also make an agreement with the child in advance about the way in which you will celebrate with him or her once they have succeeded in collecting a given number of signs in the calendar for dry mornings.

It is important to help the child understand how their bladder works. Explain to your child, with the help of a drawing, how the brain and the bladder are connected to each other with nerves. Your drawing of a human being should show the brain in the head, the pee container, the bladder, in the lower abdomen, and a nerve connecting the two. The bladder should have some sort of valve or tap which can be opened and closed by the brain. The brain is responsible for opening the valve when a person goes to the toilet and for keeping the valve tightly closed at other times, including the night. The reason children sometimes wet the bed is that the child sleeps so soundly that the brain forgets to inform the bladder to keep the valve in its closed position.

When the child understands how their brain controls the gate of their bladder, you can engage your child in a conversation about how the child can teach their bladder gate to stay closed all night till the morning. Your child can do it by using some form of self-hypnosis or affirmation; before falling asleep, when their eyes are already closed, they can, for example, let their brain speak to their bladder and repeat 3 times something along the lines of, "My dear bladder valve, please remember to stay closed all night so that I can go to the toilet to pee when I wake up in the morning!"

* * *

If you have read this far, you have by now probably formed a pretty good understanding of what I mean when I speak about the skills approach to parenting. I may have succeeded in confirming your own thinking or in inspiring you to see your child's development with new eyes. In any case, I hope I have succeeded in awakening your desire to try the approach with your own child. To this end, I conclude the book with a few useful hints that will hopefully help you avoid common pitfalls as you set out to put the ideas into practice in your own family.

Photo by Aman Shrivastava on Unsplash

8

THINGS TO KEEP IN MIND

*The best way to help children overcome challenges
is to collaborate with them.*

DOI: 10.4324/9781003435723-8

I f, after reading this book, you have become inspired by the skills approach and you feel like putting the approach into practice with your own child, or a child you care for, you may benefit from the following few practical reminders.

1. Establish a connection with the child first

The skills approach is founded on collaboration with the child. For the approach to work, you need to start by connecting with the child. There are many ways you can do this. You can, for example, pick a good moment for the conversation, then you prepare your child in some way for a conversation; or you can start by praising them for their good qualities. A good way to connect with your child before talking with them about skills to learn is to start the conversation by talking with your child about the many skills they have already learned and become better at. It is easier for children to accept the idea that there is one or more skills they might benefit from learning if you first talk about the various skills that they have already managed to develop.

2. Make sure the child wants to learn the skill

"How do I get my child to agree to learn the skill I would want him or her to learn?" is a question that I often hear when I speak to parents or educators about the skills approach. I have often presented this same question to people who have told me stories of how they have used the approach with their own children. Here are some examples of answers that I have heard from them:

> "We have two biological children and one foster child. We solved the problem by deciding that all of us, not only our foster child but also our two other children as well as me and my husband, all had a skill to learn. I think it was much easier for our foster child to go along with the idea of learning a skill when it was not only something she had to do, but something that we were all doing."

"I knew my daughter would not agree to learn the skill that I wanted her to learn, so I first let her choose another skill that she was keen on learning. Only when she had already learned the skill she had picked herself, and we had celebrated her success, I proposed that she learn the skill that I wanted her to learn. At that point she was ready to say 'yes,' but I don't think it would have worked if I had started with trying to persuade her to learn the skill I wanted her to learn."

"I chose a good moment to talk about skills to learn. We were driving to visit my mom and we, my son and I, were both in a good mood. I started by talking about some of the skills that he has already learned before I said a word about the skill that I wanted him to learn. I think it is important to pay attention to timing. I think I succeeded in picking a good moment in time to bring up the idea."

"I knew that if I would tell my daughter that I would want her to learn the skill that I was thinking of, she would not go for it. I had tried many times before to talk about the issue and she had rejected me every time. So, I decided to do it differently. I told her father, my ex-husband, about the skills approach and about the skill that I wanted our daughter to learn. Luckily, he agreed with me that it was an important skill for our daughter to develop. I reminded him of the fact that our daughter adores him and that she might be more willing to agree to learn the skill if the proposal came from him rather than me. He agreed to talk to her, and it worked. I think in our case it was better that the proposal came from her father rather than me."

"I went home after the workshop and told my son about what I had learned. I showed him some pictures and explained to him the idea that children can overcome all kinds of challenges by learning skills. Then I asked him if he wanted to help me to learn to use the approach, that is, if he would be willing to allow me to try the approach with him. He readily agreed and once he had said 'yes' to the idea, it was no longer difficult to find an agreement about a skill for him to learn."

The old saying "You can lead a horse to water, but you can't make it drink" applies to children. We cannot force children to learn what we want them to learn, but we can raise their interest in learning, not unlike feeding a horse a bit of salt to make it thirsty enough to want to drink some water from the river.

3. Make sure the skill is not stopping undesired behaviour

I often emphasise (once again) that to use the skills approach, you should make sure that when you talk about a skill to learn, you always talk about learning to act in a *desired manner* rather than learning to stop acting in an *undesired manner*. If, for example, a child should learn not to speak with his mouth full of food, the skill to learn should not be defined as "I will learn not to speak with my mouth full of food," but as something along the lines of "I will learn to wait till my mouth is empty before I speak," or if a child needs to learn not to get into fights with other children, the skill should not be defined as "I will stop getting fighting with other children," but, for example, as "I will learn to put my hands in my pockets and walk away if I get cross with other children." In other words, make sure that when talking about skills, you always talk about the things you want your child to learn to do rather than the undesired things that you would want your child to stop doing.

4. Make sure the skill is something that the child can do or say

When parents first start thinking about what skills their child would need to learn, they often initially think of high-level skills that are too broad for children to understand. Parents may say, for example, that they think their child needs to "have more self-confidence," "develop better self-control," "have a better attitude," or "have more empathy." It is difficult for children to comprehend such abstract and high-level adult language because such words do not give them clues as to what exactly they are expected to learn to do or say. For children to be able to learn skills, the skills need to be concrete — something that can be role plays, demonstrated and preferably even recorded on video. Only when the skill is concrete enough to be acted out, it becomes possible for the child to show it, to practise it and to get positive feedback from other people for their effort and progress.

5. Make sure there is an agreement about reminding

For the skills approach to work, it is important to not forget to make an agreement with the child about how you, and other people, will remind them of their skill when they sometimes forget it. You might say to your child something along the lines of, "Darling, what sign, gesture, or code do you want us to use to remind you of your skill when you sometimes forget it?" The idea is to get your child to collaborate with you in drawing up a plan for how to deal with setbacks, or occasional slip-ups, in a reassuring and supportive manner that is consistent with the skills approach.

6. Be prepared for challenges

Skills orientation is not a cure-all for all children's challenges. Putting the approach to practice is often fun and rewarding, but it can also be challenging and arduous. The child's initial interest may fade, new and unexpected problems may appear, collaboration with other adults may not be as easy as one would have hoped, and so on. Most of the time such obstacles are surmountable, but it is good to know that if the skills approach alone is not sufficient, it can always be combined with other approaches and solutions.

Photo by Austrian National Library on Unsplash

9

SKILLS APPROACH IN SCHOOLS

The skills approach improves the atmosphere of the school and reinforces collaboration between everyone.

DOI: 10.4324/9781003435723-9

I have so far in this book focused on describing how parents can apply the skills approach to support the development of their children, but it has surely become evident that also teachers and other educators can benefit greatly from adopting the skills approach in their day-to-day communication with the students and caretakers alike.

A teacher said that learning about the skills approach had changed her way of talking to her students. "Before," she said, "if a student was late, I would approach her and ask her, 'Why are you 15 minutes late again?' and that got me nowhere. Nowadays I start the conversation differently. Rather than confronting them about being late, I ask them, 'What can you do to be a little less late tomorrow?' It may sound silly, but by initiating the conversation in this way the student responds differently and we end up having a good talk about the issue."

Collaboration with students

Let's look at how the skills approach can be used to tackle the increasingly common problem of students' disruptive behaviour in class. Disruptive behaviour can take many forms. I found on an Internet forum a post submitted by a student listing various ways to act disruptively in class. The list included the following items:

- Laughing
- Giggling
- Talking with a classmate
- Shouting
- Telling the teacher off
- Rampaging
- Sending notes
- Not doing one's homework
- Spying in exams
- Answering always "I don't know" or "Beats me"
- Whistling
- Singing
- Talking to oneself
- Drumming

- Fiddling with phone
- Daydreaming in class
- Ripping up important papers
- Swinging on the chair
- Drawing on the desk surface
- Making drawings on the pages of books
- Breaking stuff
- Swearing
- Flipping the finger
- Deliberately disturbing the teacher
- Leaving the classroom without permission
- Reading and sending texts
- Talking on the phone
- Watching TikTok videos

A common teacher's response to students' disruptive behaviour is what could be called "*the consequences approach.*" According to this approach the teacher would, for example, give the student a warning, dismiss them from the classroom, inform their caretakers, seat them in the front row, send them to the principal's office, or order them detention. The consequences approach may appear reasonable, but as all teachers know it doesn't work very well and there is a considerable risk that it has a negative rather than positive influence on the student's behaviour.

A teacher using the skills approach would approach the disruptive student differently. He or she would assume that deep down the student does not want to behave in a disruptive manner and that the student would want to change their behaviour if they only knew how.

Here is a step-by-step suggestion of how the teacher might apply the skills approach to tackle the problem.

1. Reserve some time to talk with the student privately.

2. If you are annoyed or irritated, find a way to calm down before you talk to the student.

3. Start the conversation by talking with the student about their strengths; things they are good at and positive character traits they can be proud of.

4. Don't tell the student immediately why you want to talk with him or her. Ask them instead, to guess why you want to talk with them. If the student guesses correctly, you can praise them for understanding that they have room for improvement in terms of their behaviour.

5. Don't ask the student why they behave the way they do. Such typical adult questions, in the ears of students, sound like reprimands. Students don't usually know why they behave the way they do and therefore experience why-questions as frustrating.

6. Instead of describing the student's disturbing behaviour in detail, talk to them about how you would want them to act in those situations in which they have tended to behave in a disruptive manner. For example, "What could you do instead of chatting with other students during class?" or "What would help you stay in your own place?" or "What could you do instead of starting to drum on your desk?" Let the student think about a better way to act in situations in which they have had the habit of acting disruptively.

7. Changing behavioural habits is not easy. Assume that the student will not be able to make changes to his or her behaviour without the help and support of other people. Ask the student to think about how some of their classmates and their other teachers, in addition to you, can help and support them, that is, how other people can give them positive feedback for progress and remind them in some friendly way of desirable behaviour when they forget to behave in the desirable manner.

8. Keep your eyes on the student's progress and give them positive feedback even for small signs of progress. Remember to thank the student's classmates and other teachers for their support and encouragement. If possible, inform the student's parents of the positive changes, giving a good reason to feel proud of their child.

A YouTube video with me explaining this step-by-step approach is available on my YouTube channel (https://youtu.be/NLyXgD38bJo).

The skills approach increases the likelihood that the conversation with the student becomes constructive. When the focus is not on the problem but on the skill that the student is expected to learn, it is also sensible to look back and to talk with the student about some of the times he or she has managed the skill. Supposing the problem is tardiness, the teacher might say, for example, "You've come to school twice this week on time. How did you manage it? What did you do that helped you to be on time? Did someone help you, or did you do it all by yourself? I'm sure your parents will be happy when I tell them you've started to make some progress."

Collaboration with parents

The skills approach can help teachers become more successful in their communication not only with students, but also with parents. Conventionally, when students have any kind of problems at school, teachers simply inform the parents of the problem and expect them to be able to take the information to heart and do something to correct the issue. The drawback of this seemingly sensible approach is that it tends to put parents on the defensive.

For example, if the teacher informs a mother that her son has an attitude problem and talks rudely back to the teacher at school, the mother may feel blamed or criticised and respond accordingly. She may, for example, start to defend her son

- I know he's not the only one. Why are you picking on him of all the kids?
- I think you need to be more understanding towards him. He has ADHD and he's presently going through a rough time because I'm in the process of divorcing my husband.

or she may turn the blame onto someone else

- I do my best to teach him good behaviour, but his father has an awful influence on him.
- I wonder why he speaks so rudely to you because he never speaks rudely to any of the other teachers at school.

The skills approach works better than the conventional "inform-the-parents" approach because it does not prompt the parents to become defensive. When the teacher does not simply inform the parents of their child's problem behaviour but focuses instead on skills that the child might benefit from learning, the parents will find it easier to collaborate with the teacher in figuring out ways to help the child develop the skills they lack.

Put yourself in the shoes of a mother whose son's teacher contacts her and talks to her about her son's behaviour problem applying the skills approach. The teacher might say to her something along the lines of, "Your son is smart and popular among his peers, but there is a skill that I think he would benefit from learning. He can sometimes appear rude in the way he speaks to people, and I think he would benefit from learning to express himself in a more polite and considerate manner. What do you think? Would you agree that this would be a useful skill for him to learn?"

Approaching the parents with the skills approach teachers can avoid blaming or criticising the parents. Shifting the focus from problems to skills makes it easier for the parents to engage in a constructive conversation with the teacher about how to best help the student improve the skills they need to become better at.

Working with the whole class

Teachers and other educators can benefit from using the skills approach in their day-to-day conversations with students and their caretakers, but the approach can also be used with the entire class to improve the atmosphere of the class.

I have compiled, with the help of some colleagues and teachers, a template for a skills-oriented project that is called *Skilful Class*. It is a game-like process in which students develop essential social skills by helping and supporting each other.

The project starts with the teacher offering the class an opportunity to take part in the Skilful Class challenge. At this point the students do not know what the project exactly entails, but they are told that if they succeed in the challenge, there will be a festive celebration with parents in which the principal of the school will award the class with an impressive Skilful Class Certificate.

Assuming that the students become interested in the Skilful Class project, the teacher explains to them that they will need permission from the head teacher to do the project. To obtain the permission they need to write an application in which they ask the head teacher for approval to do the project. The teacher will give instructions to the class only after the class has gotten the green light from the head teacher.

The Skilful Class project consists of two separate phases. The aim of the first phase is for the pupils to demonstrate to their teacher that they understand the idea of the project and that they are capable developing skills by supporting and helping each other. The teacher explains to the class that they can choose one of six skills that they will collaboratively learn or become better at. The six optional skills are:

1. We can manage our homework

2. We can calm down for lessons

3. We can solve our disagreements and conflicts on our own

4. We can raise our hand to ask for permission to talk

5. We can listen attentively to our teachers when he or she give us instructions

6. We can ensure that we have all our necessary belongings at school

When the pupils have come to an agreement about one of these skills that they intend to become good at, the teacher divides the class into skills teams, or groups of three to four students whose task is to help and support each other in learning the skill. The teacher explains that each skill team will need to plan how to support and help each other along the way, how to praise each other when they perform the skill, and how they remind each other when they forget the skill.

When the students and the teacher agree that the class has learned the skill, or made enough progress, the teacher reveals the instructions for the next phase of the project.

In the second phase of the project each student will choose a personal skill to become better at. To help the students find a skill to learn, the teacher presents them with 22 skills of which each student can pick one they want to work on. The skills are depicted on picture cards which include the following skills:

1. I can eat neatly
2. I can say 'sorry'
3. I can help others
4. I can give compliments
5. I can encourage others
6. I can ask for help
7. I can be proud of my accomplishments
8. I can lose in games
9. I can accept that I sometimes fail and make mistakes
10. I can say "no" when needed
11. I can shift from one activity to another
12. I can talk before the class
13. I can listen to others without interrupting them
14. I can stay on task
15. I can wait for my turn
16. I can accept that I cannot always get what I want
17. I can verbally defend myself if someone teases me
18. I can ask nicely if I want something
19. I can thank others
20. I can join others
21. I can move about calmly
22. I can protect others if anyone teases them

The teacher goes through the list of skills with the students, helping them to understand what mastering each of them means in practice. Once the students are familiar with all the 22 skills, they can decide for themselves which one they want to pick to become better at. When the students have made their choice, they are instructed to make a plan in their skills team about how to help each other to ensure that everyone learns their skill. The teacher explains that the plan should include an agreement about how the students will observe each other's progress, how they will praise each other, and how they will remind each other of their skills when needed. The teacher's duty is to ensure that the project remains active, and that follow-up takes place at regular intervals.

When both the students and the teacher agree that the students have learned their skills – or made enough progress – the pre-planned celebration takes place. During the celebration the head teacher presents awards the class with the Skilful Class certificate and the students are given a chance to tell the audience how they have managed to develop their skills and, even more importantly, how they have succeeded in helping and supporting each other along the way.

Outcome research that has been conducted on The Skilful Class project in Finland as well as Russia and China, has demonstrated that the running the project has favourable effects among other things on class atmosphere, students' collaboration, and teachers' work satisfaction.

You can find more information about the Skilful Class project on my YouTube channel where I have compiled a separate playlist of videos only about this topic. A package containing the picture cards of all the skills with detailed instructions of how to conduct the Skilful Class project is available from the Helsinki Brief Therapy Institute web shop (https://shop.lti.fi)

* * *

Schools all over the Western world are struggling with many challenges including students' increasingly common behaviour problems, school avoidance, extra demanding caretakers, and teacher burnout. Replacing conventional means of intervention with the skills approach can help schools reverse their downward spiral and generate school cultures that are characterised by respectful collaboration, optimism, and creative problem solving.

AFTERWORD

Now that you are familiar with the skills approach, you will probably have realised that the approach is not a method to be applied slavishly, but a lens that makes you see people in a different light. When viewing the world through this lens, instead of seeing a multitude of people with flaws and problems around us, we see people who have stumbled upon challenges and who are capable of overcoming those challenges by learning skills with the help and support of other people.

The skills approach does not bow to authority. It does not subscribe to the view that experts know how parents should raise their children, or what they should do when their child has this or that problem. All children are different – as are all parents – and therefore well-meaning expert advice may not fit you or your child.

The skills approach is not a method. It's rather a smorgasbord. It's a compilation of child-friendly and community-oriented tools that help you to support your child to overcome challenges thereby improving the quality of life for your child, yourself, and your family.

LINKS AND RESOURCES

My related books

Kids'Skills in Action. A solution-focused method for coaching children to overcome difficulties. Originally published in 2010 by St Luke's Innovative Resources, Bendigo, Australia. Currently available also as an e-book on Amazon.

Kids'Skills. Playful and practical solution-finding with children. Published in 2004 by St Luke's Innovative Resources, Bendigo, Australia. Also available in e-book format. Download link available on the publisher's website.

Never Too Late to Have a Happy Childhood. Originally published in English in 1998 by Brief Therapy Press, London. The book has also been published in Finnish, German, French, Swedish, Chinese, Czech and Hebrew.

Kids'Skills Workbook. Helsinki Brief Therapy Institute. Helsinki 2000. A workbook for children illustrated by the renowned Finnish artist Kai Kujasalo. Available through Helsinki Brief Therapy Institute web shop which is reachable via www.brieftherapy.fi

Nigel's Nightmare. An illustrated story for parents and children about a boy whose grandmother taught him a cool trick of overcome nightmares. Available in book form in German, Finnish, and Romanian. The story is available in English for free in electronic form at www.kidsskills.org.

Dan Did Wrong. An illustrated story for parents and children about a boy who stole some money from his father and whose parents gave him an opportunity to take responsibility for his action. The story is available in English for free in electronic form at www.kidsskills.org.

Linda Tames Her Tiger. An illustrated story for parents and children about a girl whose grandfather taught her how to overcome her tantrums. Available in book form in Finnish, German, and Romanian. The story is available in English for free in electronic form at www.kidsskills.org.

Internet resources

www.kidsskills.org
A website dedicated to the Kids'Skills method and related information.

www.kidsskills.org/bully-eng
Witty Winnie: An app that you can use with your child to help them learn to respond to verbal bullying with wit and humour.

www.kidsskills.org/ocd-eng
Anxious Andy – Worry Buster App: An app that you can use with your child to help them overcome imaginary worries.

www.benfurman.com
My own website

www.youtube.com/benfurmantv
My YouTube channel

https://courses.benfurman.com
My online courses platform. Sign up to get free access to my online video course on solution-focused parenting.

https://www.kidsskillsacademy.com
An online platform offering an extensive video-based training program that allows students to become certified as a Kids'Skills coach.

Some relevant research articles

Gohier, F. M. *A support team's experience of a solution-focused intervention with children*. Master's thésis, McGill University, 2006.

Hautakangas, M., Kumpulainen, K., and Uusitalo, L. Children developing self-regulation skills in a Kids'Skills intervention programme in Finnish early childhood education and care. *Early Child Development and Care* 2021; ahead of print, 1–17.

Köhler, D., Kitta, P., Josupeit, C., and Josupeit J. "ich schaff's": Pilot-Evaluation eines systemisch-integrativen Beratungsprogramms in der Schulsozialarbeit [A pilot evaluation of a systemic-integrative counselling program in school social work]. *Familiendynamik* 2022; 47(1): 32–43.

Shuanghong, J. N., and Niemi, H. Teachers support of students' social-emotional and self-management skills using a solution-focused skilful-class method. *The European Journal of Social & Behavioural Sciences* 2020; 27(1): 3096–3114.

Shuanghong, J. N., Niemi, H., and Furman, B. Supporting children's sustainable growth with skills mindset using the solution-focused Kids'Skills method. *Sustainability* 2022; 14.

White, M. Pseudo-encopresis: From avalanche to victory, from vicious to virtuous cycles. *Family Systems Medicine* 1984; 2(2): 150–160.

Some related approaches of interest

Lawrence Cohen. *Playful parenting: An exciting new approach to raising children that will help you nurture close connections, solve behavior problems, and encourage confidence.* New York: Ballantine books, 2001.

Howard Glasser. *Transforming the difficult child: The nurtured heart approach.* Tucson: Nurtured heart Association, 1999.

Haim Omer. *Courageous parents: Becoming a good anchor for your children.* Independently published 2021.

Ross Greene. *The explosive child. A new approach for understanding and parenting easily frustrated, chronically inflexible children.* New York: Harper, 2021.

Michael White and Alice Morgan. *Narrative therapy with children and their families.* Adelaide: Dulwich Centre publications, 2006.

Jane Nelsen. *Positive discipline: The classic guide to helping children develop self-discipline, responsibility, cooperation and problem-solving skills.* New York: Ballantine books, 1981.

INDEX

Printed in the USA
CPSIA information can be obtained
at www.ICGtesting.com
LVHW011204141123
763814LV00020B/92